You Want WHAT???

Cover design by John Kasperowicz and Annie Manning

Book design and text composition by HERIBERT C BT., www.heribertc.hu

ISBN-13    978-0-9832366-0-3

Library of Congress Control Number: 2011900026

Printed in the United States

# YOU WANT WHAT???

## Concierge Tales from the Men and Women Who Make Las Vegas Dreams Come True

**Mariann Mohos**

# Contents

# Introduction

When people ask me what I do for a living and I tell them I'm a concierge, they are immediately intrigued. "Oh, I bet you have some fun stuff going on!" they exclaim. They become even more intrigued when I tell them where I ply my trade – Las Vegas.

Thanks to everything from the "What happens in Vegas" advertising campaign to movies like *The Hangover,* the public's interest in Las Vegas has intensified; people have an unending fascination with life on The Strip. They want to know the weirdest question I have ever heard as a Las Vegas concierge, the funniest guest request, the most memorable one, and so on.

Over the years, as I have shared stories about my career as a concierge, people would always want to hear more. This gave me the idea to go out and ask my fellow concierges about their stories, and to compile everything into a book to share it with the world.

I interviewed more than three dozen colleagues from both big and small hotels and combined them to be told here by one voice. Since a cornerstone of our profession is privacy, all guest names have been changed. A few stories have also been modified for various reasons, but all has been done to protect those involved as well as the narrative.

Interviewing my fellow Las Vegas concierges turned out to be an extremely rewarding experience. I soon learned that I definitely had not heard it all and that some requests really should be deemed too strange.

There is truly no limit to the variety of things that happen to a concierge on the Strip. In one conversation, you might be talking about where to get the best foie gras, and in the next you could be assisting a guest whose quickie marriage has turned out to be the biggest mistake of his young life. You may even find yourself meeting some famous people and doing whatever it takes to get them their coveted grilled cheese sandwiches. We concierges have found ourselves on our knees in front of Playboy bunnies and covering naked old men with pillows from the lobby. Sometimes, we use our network of connections to get things done—whether it be getting someone out of an Italian jail or finding a straightjacket on the strip. At other moments, we are there to help our guests through some of the toughest and most unexpected times—from sudden death to life-threatening injury. You never know what your role as concierge may actually involve. For the most part though, it's all about helping guests fulfill their personal and vacation dreams.

Finally, I hope that you, the reader, will have as much fun reading through these Las Vegas snippets as I did compiling them. If you happen to have a Las Vegas concierge story of your own that you would like to share, please feel free to email me at the address listed below.

At your service,

*Mariann Mohos*

*April, 2015*

*lveditors@gmail.com*

# Goofy Moments

## Not Quite Rolling a 7 or 11

People who visit Las Vegas are often star-struck by the sights, the sounds, and the amenities. Between this and the plans that are swirling around in their heads, they sometimes get distracted. Often, this can lead to silly questions or situations where guests just aren't thinking clearly. Of course, it also leads to a special kind of hilariousness!

In the so-called "City of Sin", a concierge must prepare herself for the most outrageous of requests. In preparing to accommodate the most incredible of desires (within reason and the law, of course), we often err on the side of the fantastical, even when the request is quite benign. Maybe we just aren't expecting to hear someone ask for something so boring and harmless. This over-estimating, however, has made doing the job a little harder than it needed to be a time or two.

A Scottish gentleman had been staying with us, and one morning, he called me at the concierge desk.

"Can you please find me a virgin chicken?" he asked.

Having a bit of a distracted day, I confirmed with him that I could before his request clearly registered, but when I hung up the phone and allowed myself a moment, my heart sank: what had I committed to finding? I became doubtful; but then again, this was Vegas, and he was from a different country. I steeled myself to give this man exactly what he wanted, committed to making the guests' stay the absolute best.

I consulted a few other staff members.

"Have you ever heard of someone needing a virgin chicken?" I asked. I must admit, visions of rituals and rites performed with dark hoods and golden chalices entered my mind, but I put them out of my way. I had only known this guest to be the most pleasant of men.

When none of my colleagues could help me, I did what any good concierge would do: I Googled the term. Needless to say, the search results were off the wall and in some cases, positively X-rated.

I was rather embarrassed, because for the most part, Vegas concierges have at least a 'working knowledge' of anything a guest could ask for. We've seen it all and heard it all. So it was with regret that I called the guest and told him that we couldn't find a virgin chicken anywhere. That's when we discovered that the man's thick Scottish accent had been a problem.

He'd asked for a "Virgin check-in," as in Virgin Atlantic Airlines. He jetted back home after some gentle ribbing of the staff member who had taken his first call, and no doubt shared this story with glee back in Glasgow. Who can blame him?

Now, I consider myself adept at reading people, and so I resolved that this guest had no intention of using a virgin chicken for any of the purposes Google thought to mention.

Suddenly, I snapped my fingers in inspiration: it must be some delicacy he'd like to enjoy while he was here. I began calling a few of the finer restaurants on the Strip.

"Am I being pranked?" one chef asked me. "Is this some weird episode of 'Punked'?" he accused.

"No, no," I assured him. "I just had a question about a virgin chicken from a guest, and I wasn't really sure what it meant. Is it some dish, or some special delicacy?"

Chef after chef laughed at my inquiry, but I was bound and determined to find this guest his unadulterated bird!

I was rather embarrassed because, for the most part, Vegas concierges have at least a 'working knowledge' of anything a guest could ask for. We've seen it all and heard it all. So it was with regret that I called the guest to give him the bad news.

"I have to admit that I've failed to accommodate you," I said to him. "I've exhausted my resources, but I cannot find a virgin chicken anywhere."

"Chicken?" he repeated. "No, no chicken. To fly—on Virgin Atlantic."

My palm went to my forehead immediately, and I realized the problem: the thick Scottish accent had thrown me for a loop. No poultry was necessary or even desired. He'd asked for a "Virgin check-in," for Virgin Atlantic Airlines.

"That, sir, is not a problem," I assured him, and began to process the request. I'm sure that he jetted back home, and no doubt shared this story with glee back in Glasgow—telling his friends of the poor concierge who spent half the day trying to locate a virgin chicken.

But, hey—those are some of the lengths we concierges will go to. All in the name of customer service!

• • •

Speaking of customer service, it's not uncommon for guests to realize they miss certain creature comforts from home or find out that they forgot to pack certain items and call us for help. I've gotten calls from our guests needing anything from bull testicles to a sewing kit to breast milk and beyond. Most of these necessities easily translate from one culture to another, from the mother-tongue to English. There was, however, this one time I can recall when I found myself Lost in Translation.

The phone rang at my desk, and I answered it cheerily. The guest on the other end said, "Can I have a tubastic sent to my room?"

I thought I had misunderstood him because I was certain I didn't know what a tubastic was.

"I'm sorry, sir. I didn't quite catch what you said. Can you repeat that?"

"Please can I have a tubastic sent to my room?"

I remember squinting then, as if that might help me visualize the unknown word or somehow help me to translate what he was saying. Wracking my brain and going through the most commonly forgotten items, I made an attempt to get him what he needed.

"Toothpaste?" I questioned.

"Yes," the voice on the other end said. "Yes, please."

Relieved that I'd figured out what he needed—and feeling good that it didn't take too many guesses— I told the guest that I would have someone bring it up to his room immediately.

I employed the bellman to run my errand. I was busy making dinner reservations for another guest and his wife, so I didn't expect it when the man came down a few minutes later with the bellman who'd just taken the toothpaste up to him. I watched him hurry across the lobby's expansive white marbled floor, bellman hot on his heels trying to keep up.

The guest pointed to the toothpaste. "I need a tubastic," he said. "Not this. A tubastic."

I was at a loss, and had no idea what to do. Even with the man here in front of me so that I could hear him clearly and watch his lips move, I still had no idea what a tubastic was.

"Tubastic," I repeated the word. It was a word that had no meaning to me, and the rate I was going, it never would.

"Tubastic," the guest repeated, and he began to point to his mouth and make an in and out movement with his hand. I was trapped in this horrible game of charades where all I could think was, "Tubastic? What's a tubastic? What does he need?"

I decided I'd just go through a list of possibilities. "Do you need a toothbrush, sir?"

His eyes lit up and he nodded. "Yes," he said, reassuringly. So I handed him a cellophane-wrapped toothbrush.

"Here you are, sir."

He looked at it and began to shake his head. "No. A tubastic," he repeated.

I was beginning to hate the sound of the word.

He opened his mouth again and moved his hand in and out.

I hadn't been on the job that long, and I didn't want to give any hotel guests any reason to be disgruntled with my services. I could see, however, that the guest's frustrations were escalating, as were my own, but for the life of me I couldn't figure out what it was.

"Do you need me to call a dentist?" I asked, but he shook his head no and repeated that infernal word, tubastic, while still making the odd movement with his hand towards his mouth.

Then something shifted. It was the slightest of motions, but it was enough to ignite the lightbulb above my head.

"Oh! You need a toothpick!" I practically screamed at the guest.

"Yes! Yes!" he nodded emphatically, and when I handed him the small, individually wrapped toothpicks (giving him a few extra for good measure), he peeled it from its wrapper, stuck it between his teeth, and walked away smiling. I think both of us felt we had come out winners on that one.

● ● ●

As a concierge in a city like Las Vegas, we often get some interesting questions. Of course, since I live in Las Vegas, not a lot fazes me, but what may seem mundane to me is often mind-blowing to my guests. Sometimes, too, we all get a little caught up in our own little world.

Not long ago, a guest came to my desk. "I'm trying to get tickets to a show, but I'm not sure how it's spelled."

"What's the name of the show, sir?" I asked kindly.

"O," he replied.

"O," I answered.

"Yes. That's the one. How do you spell it?" he asked.

"O," I replied.

"Yes. That's the show I'd like to see. I was going to buy my tickets online, see, but I'm not sure how to spell it," he tried to clarify.

"It's O," I answered.

The guest thought for a minute, cocked his head to the side, and then frowned. "O?"

"Yep. That's how you spell it. Just the letter. Nothing fancy."

I saw the mental slap to the forehead he was giving himself as he blushed, mumbled his appreciation, and walked away embarrassed.

But it's okay; this sort of thing happens all the time. Believe it or not, I've had more than one guest ask me what time it's going to rain tomorrow, and if it does rain, undoubtedly, a few people will stop by my desk to ask me when it will stop raining. I've even had a guest ask, "Will it rain in October?"

What I love about these questions is just how much my guests believe I know or can do. Think of the power they think I wield!

I remember fondly one particular surgeon who'd come to Las Vegas for a convention. On the day of his departure, he called down to my desk in a bit of a panic.

"I'm running late," he informed me. "I need some help."

"Certainly," I responded, ready to accommodate this guest and his schedule.

"Can you get on the phone with the airline and tell them they're going to have to hold the plane?" he asked me.

At first, I thought he was joking, and I have to admit that I let a slight giggle escape. When I heard a heavy stillness on the other end of the line, I realized with a sinking feeling that he was indeed very serious.

"I'm so sorry," I began, "I thought you were kidding around with me."

"This is not a joke. There's no way I'm going to make my flight," he explained. "I just need you to tell them that I'm on my way, and to hold that flight."

"Sir, it's not that I'm not willing to do anything to accommodate you, but the airlines just aren't going to hold the plane. They don't do that. In all my years working with the airlines, I've never had them hold a flight for anyone."

"I think they'll understand," he insisted. "I have to get back today, so please just get the airline on the phone. I'll be down in two minutes."

Shaking my head, I resigned myself to comply, and just as I got the representative on the phone, the guest approached the desk, his hand held out for the phone.

I handed him the receiver with a wan smile, and in a clipped business tone he introduced himself.

"This is Dr. Calloway. I'm a surgeon in New York City, and I am on flight number 827 that departs in ten minutes. I need you to hold that plane. I'm on my way, but I'll be another fifteen minutes or so."

He stood there for a few minutes, his brow furrowing as he listened. "Uh huh. Yes. Okay. I see. Thank you, then."

He handed the receiver back to me with a puzzled look on his face.

"Turns out you're right. Apparently, they don't do that sort of thing. Who'd have thought?"

● ● ●

Most of these requests happen on a regular basis each day in the life of a concierge, and believe it or not, I consider it relatively "normal" when a guest approaches my desk and asks where the porn shop is. After all, we are in Vegas, and what happens in Vegas . . . well, you know the rest.

On a typical Monday afternoon, one particular gentleman approached my desk to ask where the porn shop was. Many concierges would most likely respond with, "Sir, there are several. Take your pick," but I happened to know that there was a large porn convention in town at this time. Being the proactive concierge that I am and eager to surpass all expectations, I gave him detailed directions on how to get to the convention center that was hosting the porn gathering. He thanked me kindly and was off.

A few hours later, I saw the guest return, and I straightened my blouse when I saw him approach the desk. I figured he was coming to thank me for the stellar job I did in getting him to his destination.

"Excuse me," he said quietly as he glanced around him.

"Good evening, sir. I hope you enjoyed yourself this afternoon," I said as cheerily as I could.

He frowned and looked over his shoulder. "That's what I came to ask you about," he said quietly. "Why did you send me to a pornography convention?"

He was almost whispering the words so that I had to lean across the desk to hear him clearly.

"I'm sorry," I said, lowering my voice to match his. "Didn't you ask me where the porn shop was? I assumed you were meaning the large gathering in town. Perhaps you wanted just a shop," I said, confused.

"No. I wanted the porn shop," he repeated.

I leaned in a little more, thinking that maybe I wasn't hearing something correctly. I looked him in the eyes, but he could barely meet my gaze. I stood there confused, wondering how I could have been wrong.

"Did you want a specific shop? Do you know the name of it?" I asked.

"Yeah, I wanted that one porn shop. The one that's on television."

*Think. Think. Think*, I told myself. What Vegas porn shop is on television? He looked at my blank stare and finally ended my agony.

"It's that show, *Porn Stars*. With the granddad, the dad, and the kid all working in the shop together."

Suddenly I realized the mistake and immediately became embarrassed.

"*Pawn Stars!*" I exclaimed.

"Yes. That's what I said, *Porn Stars*. So, why did you send me to that convention?"

I began to shake my head, the laughter starting before I had a chance to explain my mistake.

"Let's just say this," I began. "I obviously misunderstood, and you obviously got more than you bargained for. That is, like, *the* largest pornography convention that comes to Vegas."

I promised then and there to get him a taxi and instruct the taxi to take him to the pawn shop, the one on the television show called *Pawn Stars* and steered him clear of any more porn stars for the rest of the visit.

• • •

I once had an older gentleman checking in who came to my desk for some details about the entertainment in Vegas.

"Well, will you be staying through Saturday?" I asked.

"What?" he asked as he leaned forward.

"Will you be staying through Saturday?" I repeated a little louder. "There are some great shows on Saturday that I can recommend."

"Oh, yes," he said.

"Wonderful," I smiled. "And are there specific acts or restaurants that you'd like to try? I can set up a great dinner and show package for you."

"What?" he said again, leaning further over my desk.

Again, I repeated myself a little louder than I had before.

In the middle of my question, he interrupted me. "You should probably know that I have AIDS," he said rather loudly.

Unaccustomed to guests volunteering information about life-threatening illnesses—especially so openly and loudly—I faltered for a second. Of course, I felt terrible, and it took me a moment to gather myself. "Oh, sir. I'm so sorry to hear that."

"What?" he asked.

I spoke up. "I said, 'I am so sorry to hear that.'"

He cocked his head to the side and looked at me quizzically. After a few beats, his furrowed brow finally smoothed out in understanding, and his eyes widened.

"No, no! Not that kind of AIDS," he said. "Hearing aids." He pointed to each of his ears and turned his head in my direction so that I could see the inconspicuous little contraptions resting inside each ear.

For the rest of our conversation, I spoke loudly, all the while keeping my laughter at myself under wraps.

• • •

One of the most popular destinations on the Strip is the Eiffel Tower experience at the Paris Hotel and Casino. This is a pay-as-you-go, self-guided tour through a half-scale replica of the famous French landmark. Of course, people wonder why it isn't the full size; after all, everything seems over the top in Vegas, so why would the Eiffel Tower be half the size of the original?

It's all logistics, you see. The airport is very close, and had the tower been built at the original dimensions, it would have easily been hit. So, the contractors settled on half the size, but it certainly doesn't take away from its glory.

One couple had inquired about the experience, but it seemed I didn't give them all the information they were hoping for.

"So how do we get to the top?" the wife asked.

"You take a glass elevator ride to the summit," I replied. "The ride itself is truly amazing, and you'll definitely want to take your camera so that when you're at the top, you can photograph the twinkling night-time tapestry of Las Vegas from there. It's magical and romantic! You're going to love it!"

We talked a little bit more about the experience, and the couple was preparing to walk away when the wife put her hand on her husband's arm, stopped, and turned to him. "Okay, so we take the elevator up, but how do we get back down?"

For a moment, I thought about suggesting his-and-hers parachute rentals, but instead I bit my tongue and smiled, allowing the woman a few moments to process her question. She actually began to giggle at herself. Then together, we nodded and assured each other that the elevator that goes up also comes down as well.

# Love and Marriage in Las Vegas

## Gambling on Love

While gambling is the number one industry in Las Vegas, weddings constitute the second largest industry. This has led to Vegas becoming known as the Marriage Capital of the world. One of the most touching things about being a concierge is getting to be a part of these intimate life moments between guests. Whether it's helping to set up the perfect proposal or ironically assisting in the creation of a divorce 'celebration,' concierges are able to witness moments that will forever change the lives of the guests involved. It can be very emotional, and most of these moments are ones that we keep close to our hearts.

It's always a pleasure to help those guests who are planning a special wedding proposal. I mean, how many people get to help make such a memorable event come together? I'm always honored to be a part of such a special and momentous occasion.

One guest I recall had been planning the perfect marriage proposal for quite some time. We had been helping him with everything since he checked in: finding the perfect roses, renting the nicest limo, going to the hottest show and booking the best restaurant for dinner. But this wasn't all he had in mind.

"What I'd really like is a gondola ride at the Venetian Hotel. Is there any way we can reserve a gondola?"

Sadly, I had to deny him. "There's no way to make a reservation," I told him. "It's first come, first served."

"Maybe I can rent out a gondola?" he asked.

I shrugged, unsure, and pointed at his itinerary. "You have a super-tight schedule," I noted. "Do you think you'd be able to estimate a time window for this?"

He bit the side of his lip. "Maybe if I talked to someone over there," he mused, "but how in the world will I get away from her long enough to try and arrange it? I'm running out of time now."

I could sense his nervousness and anxiety, but I am a hopeless romantic. I wanted to see him pull off this incredible marriage proposal just as he'd been envisioning it. An idea came to me.

"You can let me know when you think you'll be there," I suggested. "Then, I'll go and pay for the ride, and you can just reimburse me."

I was so caught up in the proposal that I couldn't stand the thought of him missing his chance to get the gondola ride. He wasn't sure how long it would take him, so I decided to err on the side of safety. I arrived at the ticket kiosk promptly at 9:00 that evening, and purchased two tickets for the 9:30 gondola ride. Aware that if he got there even just a few seconds late, he wouldn't be allowed on, I decided to go ahead and purchase tickets for the 9:40 gondola and the 9:50 as well, just in case their waiter was late with the bill or something else held the couple up.

Luckily, the couple made it in time, and he asked her to marry him during the romantic gondola ride that almost hadn't happened. She was overwhelmed and very touched, and of course she said yes.

When they entered the hotel later that evening, the bride-to-be rushed to my desk, already glowing with that wedding glow.

"Paul told me how much you helped him put everything together," she gushed. "I just want to give you a hug."

And as I walked around the desk, she enveloped me in a strong bear-hug, squeezing my neck tightly.

"Thank you," she said. "It was the most beautiful night of my entire life!"

I have to admit I had to fight the tears when I pulled back and saw her own eyes glimmering with new emotion.

"I'm just glad I could help," I said. "And that you said 'yes'. Poor Paul would have done a lot of work for a broken heart," I pointed out, smiling.

"Not me," he said. "I merely had the vision. You did the work to make it happen, and we'll always remember that."

I winked at the bride-to-be. "Seems like you've got yourself a good one," I said. "He could have easily taken all the credit for himself." I turned to Paul. "You keep all this up, and you two will most certainly live happily ever after!"

•   •   •

Most people know how joyous and exciting a marriage party or reception can be. It's a wonderful occasion, and I'm always happy when we get to hold those parties at the hotel. There's something remarkable about watching the couple dance their first dance as man and wife even after the stress and chaos of preparing for the wedding and the party. At one hotel I worked in, I learned that there's something to be said for divorce parties as well.

I've worked as a residential concierge for a couple of years and one of our permanent residents approached my desk one day.

"I need your help with a divorce party," Barbara told me.

I cocked my head to one side. I'd never heard of a divorce party.

"It'll be in my suite, but I'd love your help with some of the finer details," she said, and together we began making lists and plans. This was all something new to me, but without judgment, I threw myself into making arrangements to give her a divorce party even better than her wedding party had been. I began to think of the idea as novel and fun, a way to stay positive about something that could be viewed extremely negatively.

When the day of the party came, Barbara invited me to partake, and I couldn't help but stand in amazement at the way her vision had come together. Instead of beautiful fresh blossoms, we began with a bouquet of dying, withering flowers, symbolic of the life that she'd had with her ex-husband. These were placed in "his" former area, on the masculine mahogany desk where he had handled the bills, written a few letters, and also left the paperwork for their divorce. Also in "his" former corner were black candlesticks and low lighting to contrast with the rest of the room, which was bright and celebratory with Barbie-pink accents everywhere.

Along with that, one area of the room was lined with things that the ex-husband liked and objects that reminded her of him; from Star Wars memorabilia to football to the stacks of *Playboy* she had discovered. As a part of her grand entrance into the party, Barbara walked past all of these items, including dirty clothes she would no longer have to wash, discarded cans of cheap beer she would not have to pick up, and bags of Cheetos and Doritos representing the orange dust that had forever left her life for good. None of it would she have to endure any more. She emerged into the main area through a bunch of colorful balloons that were symbolic of her newfound freedom and the things she had already sworn to devote herself to: going on a cruise, learning to paint, playing golf.

There was certainly some humor interjected; Barbara and her friends had each contributed samples of the food her ex-husband liked, all representing dishes or meals she wouldn't have to cook anymore if she didn't want to. Ceremoniously, Barbara said a few departing words, and then one by one, they dumped them down the garbage disposal. Someone had brought a plastic toy engagement-style ring, and that was tossed down there as well, symbolizing the union which was now dissolved. When they turned on the garbage disposal, a cheer went up from all the women gathered in the room, and arms were flung wide in freedom.

Unbeknownst to Barbara, her friends had taken her former wedding ring and created a beautiful new pendant, a symbol of the transformation that Barbara had experienced.

The whole party was remarkable and quite memorable. I could feel Barbara's new sense of empowerment wafting over us all like a new perfume. It was probably then that I realized the woman emerging from the rainbow of balloons really was a new woman completely; one committed to looking forward and making the best of her life. What had started as a cute, tongue-in-cheek celebration actually became a moment of liberation for all of the women there. It was a fantastic way to acknowledge that everything in life depends on your perspective, and when it comes to love and marriage—and divorce— it's important to always remember to love yourself.

•   •   •

With easy access in Las Vegas to drive-through wedding chapels, it's the perfect spot for couples who want a fast wedding. A couple of guests had come to Vegas and thought it would be a great opportunity for them to renew their vows after twenty years of marriage. For as long as anyone can remember, Vegas has been *the* destination for those wanting to tie the knot—or retie the knot— quickly, and re-newlyweds have become as common as newlyweds in Las Vegas.

"Our family is scattered all over the United States," the wife told me, "and we toyed with the idea of having a huge renewal ceremony, but . . . well, it just seemed like a lot of money and a lot of trouble to try and get everyone here for the event."

"So," the husband continued where his wife left off (as I was sure they'd been doing for years), "we thought it'd be fun to come to Vegas and do the opposite of what we'd done twenty years ago: go to one of those drive-through wedding chapels. You know, have fun with it."

"I love it!" I encouraged. "That way, you get the best of both worlds. You've already had the big fancy wedding; now you can opt for the Vegas drive-through chapel. I'll be happy to make the arrangements for you."

I got them booked in at a nearby drive-through, and then we ordered a small cake and champagne to have ready in the lobby, vowing to celebrate with them when they returned from the renewal. They were as giddy as newlyweds as they left for their dinner reservations, all their arrangements made for the following day.

Minutes after they left, however, I received a call from Bob, the oldest son of the couple.

"Look, I know that my parents are in Vegas, and I'm also aware that they are planning to renew their vows. Do you know if they've done this yet?"

I was pleased to tell them that the date was set for tomorrow.

"Perfect," he said. "I have a sneaky surprise of my very own."

After a relatively short conversation, I hung up the phone with Bob and called the chapel where I'd just made the renewal arrangements.

"There's a slight change of plans," I told the hostess, and we began to reconfigure the celebration to accommodate Bob's own ideas for his parents' renewal.

At the appointed time the next day, the couple pulled up to the drive-through wedding chapel. As they prepared to renew their vows, they looked in the rear-view mirror (of an Elvis-style Cadillac, no less) to see swarms of bicycles coming around the corner of the chapel and lining up behind them. Finally, peering at the faces of the people on bicycles and tricycles, they recognized them as their very own children and grandchildren, all of whom had arrived to surprise their parents on their anniversary—a plan that had been in the works since their parents had said they were going to Vegas.

It was a first for the drive-through chapel, and even those working there were emotional and crying along with the couple and their children.

Once the vows were said, and the husband was instructed to kiss his wife, the kids brought out a tandem bicycle with a sign attached that read "Just Re-Married". The not-so-newlyweds rode together down the sidewalk on the Vegas Strip back to the hotel (where a much larger party had been planned and was being prepared for all the surprise guests), receiving waves and kisses and well-wishes from strangers all along the Strip.

And what had started as a small, fun celebration for the two of them had become an experience the entire family got to share in . . . and I was honored to be able to make it happen for them.

• • •

"I need your help," a guest called down and said to me one day.

"Sure. That's why I'm here," I replied cheerfully. "Now, what can I help you with?"

"I need to order twenty-four dozen roses for my room," he said.

I chuckled and asked for clarification. "Did you mean to say you wanted twenty-four roses, as in two dozen?"

"No," he said. "I meant exactly what I said: twenty-four dozen roses, as in a total of two-hundred-and-eighty-eight roses."

I let out a low whistle, but didn't answer right away, which must have made him question himself.

"Do you think that will be too overwhelming in my hotel room?"

I heard a nervous tremor in his voice at that moment, and I began to catch on to the gravity of the task.

"Well, it's a fact: twenty-four dozen roses are going to make your room look like a botanical garden!" He was in one of the smallest rooms in the hotel.

He sighed a bit into the receiver. "That's what I want," he said. "See, I'm going to propose to my girlfriend, and I want her to be overwhelmed . . . but not *too* overwhelmed."

I understood the delicate balance, and besides, the quiver in his voice and all two-hundred plus roses were just tugging at my heartstrings.

"Let me make some calls," I told him. "It may take a little work to rustle up twenty-four dozen roses, but I feel confident we can make this happen!"

His plan was to take his girlfriend out that afternoon, but they would be back by five since he had reservations for a special dinner later that evening.

"I'm hoping this will be a celebratory dinner," he confided, and I crossed my fingers for him and promised to have everything ready by the time they returned seven hours later.

I made a call to my favorite florist, and he attempted to correct me in the same way I'd tried to correct my guest.

"Nope," I said. "He really wants the 24-dozen roses."

"Geez! He'd better be glad it's close to Valentine's Day. I wouldn't have that many roses ready for him on just any day."

The bill came to just over three-thousand dollars (the biggest order that florist has received to date), and we filled the room with both long-stem and short-stem roses.

When the man and his girlfriend returned, they walked into a room that was practically painted red with roses. Those flowers were arranged on the tables, placed in the bathroom, draped across the dresser – they were everywhere!

On their way out for their celebratory dinner, they stopped by my desk.

"Thank you so much for your help," he said, the wide smile across his face evidence of his success.

The girlfriend's new diamond ring sparkled in the lighting, and I remarked on its beauty and the man's good taste as I wished them every happiness.

"We're off to paint the town red," he smiled before they left. "We had so much fun turning one room red, we figured we'd go for the whole Strip!"

●    ●    ●

I've seen a lot of men and women in uniform come to Las Vegas before or after a posting abroad. It's a popular place for making the last days at home memorable, as well as a great place to celebrate a safe, happy return. One young Navy recruit—Josh—will always hold a special place in my heart. He and his girlfriend were staying with us, and he came to me one day, explaining that he wanted to propose to his small-town sweetheart before he shipped out to Iraq.

"I've never traveled to a big city before," he confessed. "I feel like I'm a bit out of my league. But I want to make this a memorable proposal—better than she ever would have imagined."

I smiled. "That is something we can do!" I told him.

"Here's the thing," he said, nervously pulling at his collar. "I don't even have the ring yet," he smiled sheepishly. "I was hoping you could give me some advice on that, too."

I began asking him a series of questions to find out his ideas and her likes. Together, we began concocting a Vegas wedding proposal that Hollywood would have coveted. True to form, he answered everything very formally, with "Yes, ma'am," and "No, ma'am".

After a brief tutorial on the "four Cs" of purchasing a diamond, I pointed him in the direction of an affordable jeweler.

When the big night arrived, he approached the concierge desk with a nervous grin.

"Can you help me with my tie?" he asked me. His hands were shaking so badly I was certain he couldn't get the tie to cooperate. Clad in his blue Navy dress uniform, he rehearsed his proposal in a whisper as I straightened his tie and brushed off his shoulders. His heart was racing, and I could see his heartbeat in his throat. I started feeling nervous for him, but we both calmed at the sight of his girlfriend walking through the lit tree-lined lobby and across the mosaic tiled floor. She was stunning in a beautiful emerald-green evening gown, and I felt a small stab of pride at the role I had played in the big event.

Of course, she had no idea what awaited. Josh had told her that he wanted to take her to a nice restaurant, something special before he shipped out, just part of the big Vegas weekend he had planned with her before he left for Iraq.

I, on the other hand, knew that he'd picked a gorgeous ring: antique-style setting ornamented with an engraved scroll pattern on the top and sides of a perfect round diamond. The plan we'd laid was that he would propose at the restaurant, where I'd arranged for the ring to come out with the dessert. Then they would retire to their suite to celebrate with a bottle of champagne and roses. The next evening, they'd see a romantic show—their first outing as an engaged couple.

When Josh and his girlfriend came back from dinner, he was in tears. My heart stopped beating for a few seconds as I thought the worst, but when I saw the smile on his girlfriend's face, I knew they were tears of joy.

"She said 'yes,'" he told me and pulled her hand up to show off the symbol of their new betrothal. He was choked up at that point, so his girlfriend stepped in.

"Josh told me how much you helped him," she said. "Thank you for all you did to make this the best night of my life."

I looked from her eyes into Josh's, and he nodded emphatically and reached out for a hug.

I felt the tears spring to my own eyes. Here he was, so young and innocent and polite, about to go off to defend our country... it moved me.

"It was my honor," I said finally, wiping a stray tear from my cheek. "I'm happy to help, and I hope you will accept it as my own small way of supporting his bravery – both as a soldier and as a man in love!"

· · ·

We often deal with marriage proposals. The usual is a romantic dinner and a nice show, but one guest had a request that was out of the ordinary, and what started out as a fairytale turned into a nightmare more quickly than anticipated.

I'd been working as a concierge for twelve years when a guest named Ethan approached me. He told me he'd been living with his girlfriend Chloe for sixteen years, and he was ready to finally get married.

"The catch is this: I'm really nervous about asking," he said. "I mean, I know we've been together forever, but . . . well, when you finally pop the question, there's just no guarantee she'll say 'yes.'"

"How can I help you with this?" I asked him with a smile.

"I want the entire proposal and wedding here, in Las Vegas." He further explained that they'd be coming from Australia. "Your mission—should you choose to accept—is to plan the entire wedding."

My mouth dropped open in shock and confusion. "Plan the wedding?" I squeaked.

He confirmed and elaborated that it would all be a surprise, so he wanted me to plan her entire wedding with no input from her at all.

*You have GOT to be kidding me!* I thought at first. I may not know much about weddings, but I did know that a woman's wedding day is one of the most important days of her life!

"You want me to arrange the entire wedding—minister, cake, rings, everything?" I asked.

"Yes," he said. "We'll get married in the room, something beautiful yet simple – nothing fancy."

I was incredulous. "But what about the dress?"

He replied, "You'll choose it. I'll give you the size and some ideas of dresses she would like."

I felt my pace quicken, and the blood drained from my face. I couldn't believe this was actually happening, that this man was really asking me this.

But he was, and so I began planning his secret surprise wedding.

The process took about four weeks, with calls and emails back and forth between myself and Ethan. After choosing the flowers, the minister, and other little details, I finally narrowed my dress search down to three contenders. I sent him a picture of each, to which he replied, "Well, I really don't know that much about dresses, which is why I wanted you to choose."

I was hoping to at least have him pick one of the three as his personal favorite or at least give me an idea of which one he thought Chloe would like best, but no. Everything was left up to me.

The one aspect he did help me with was selecting a jazz musician. (Hey, at least it was something.) Since Chloe loved jazz so much, we settled on a jazz player for the ceremony and began finalizing all of the plans as the date got closer.

I have to admit, I was starting to feel nervous—and I wasn't even the one who had to propose! It turned out that shortly after the couple checked into the hotel, Chloe got very sick with the flu. Since they were scheduled to be at the hotel for a week, I was able to push all the arrangements back, and I sent the in-house doctor to her.

"Please, Doc," I begged the doctor, "do whatever it takes to make this woman better! I can't keep myself and her soon-to-be-fiancé hanging in the balance much longer."

He pumped her full of antibiotics and a few vitamin shots, and two days later, she began to feel better. Everything was back on, and so I finalized the reservations for Ethan so that he could propose.

The moment arose, and when he finally asked her for her hand, she burst into tears. "I came all the way here from Australia, not to mention that I've been sick," she said. "I've been living with you for sixteen years, and *now* you're asking to get married? Here?" Chloe stopped long enough to catch her breath before launching into her attack again. "You knew I wanted to do this at home, with my family around me. What were you thinking? This is the opposite of the type of proposal and wedding I would *ever* want. Ever!"

I couldn't believe it when he told me all this—though I'd had my qualms and worries at the beginning. I just kept thinking about all the work we'd done to get this ready. And, of course, his broken heart.

"So what did you tell her?" I asked.

Ethan shrugged. "What could I say? I told her I'd simply wanted it to be a surprise, something she'd remember for the rest of her life, something completely unexpected. I wanted to save her the stress and work. I had done everything with the best of intentions."

"And so?" I prompted.

He hung his head. "She told me, 'Good intentions or not, no way. Absolutely not.'"

I felt awful. I think I was as crushed as he was over the whole thing—but for an entirely different reason, of course. "I'm so sorry," I whispered, but he looked up into my eyes.

"I'm not giving up yet," he told me.

The next day, Chloe came down to the lobby and headed straight for my desk. I saw her walking the length of the long service desk, and I tried to read the expression on her face to prepare myself for our encounter. She could easily want to tell me how stupid I was to go along with Ethan's plan, that as a woman I should understand the sacredness of planning out one's own wedding.

"I'm glad to see you are feeling better," I said honestly, hoping to start the conversation off on the right foot.

She smiled a thin smile and then said, "I heard that you picked out my wedding dress."

I cleared my throat to buy a little time as my mind raced. "Yes," I mumbled. I could feel myself beginning to sweat, my armpits dampening against me.

"I'd like to see it," she said.

"Absolutely." I took her to the storage area where the dress was hanging. As I unzipped the garment bag and pulled the dress out, her eyes widened.

I wasn't sure if she was having a positive reaction or a negative one. She stared at the dress for a long time, and then finally, she said, "This is unbelievable. I love it! This is exactly the dress I would have chosen."

We stood there—me sweating and her running her hands over every detail of the dress. The silence was awkward and uncomfortable, yet I preferred it to the verbal attack I had anticipated from her. After a few more seconds, still looking at the dress dreamily, she said, "You know what? I'm going to do it. I'm going to get married in Las Vegas."

"What?" I asked.

She turned to face me. "Why not? It's a great surprise, after all. We can do this here and do something at home with my family too. Who's to say Ethan can't have his dream, and I can't have mine too?"

And just like that, the wedding was on again. It was just the couple, the minister, and me as the witness. We stood in their plush white and beige hotel room, the minister's back to the panoramic view of Las Vegas as he intoned the vows. It was a magical setting, the lights of Vegas just coming up since it was dusk.

As I stood listening to the two exchange vows, I realized Las Vegas had a new roller coaster this week: this whole thing had been an absolute emotional ride, and if that's what it had been like for me, I could only imagine what it'd been like for the couple: up and then down and then up again.

Ethan and Chloe still return to Las Vegas to celebrate an anniversary every now and then, and they always find me. I was so happy that everything worked out, and I decided I learned one important lesson about myself during this whole process: if I ever decide against being a concierge, at least I have a promising future as a secret wedding planner.

• • •

I got a call from a guest who was bringing his wife to Vegas to celebrate their thirtieth wedding anniversary.

"I want to do something very special," he said, and he proceeded to give me a few detailed requests.

First, he wanted twelve dozen roses in the room. "Each dozen must be a different color," he instructed, and I assured him that we would have no problem fulfilling that request.

"Secondly, I need a violinist and an accordion player to play a concert in the room for a few hours." He'd already booked our two-thousand-square-foot suite for the weekend, and I was beginning to concoct a plan to make their stay a trip down memory lane, but now I was wondering how I would find a violinist and an accordionist who could play together, much less who could have time to compile and rehearse a short concert for a guest who was arriving in a matter of weeks.

"The third thing I'd like is one of the cocktail waitress uniforms," the guest said.

"You mean like a costume?" I asked.

"No. Like one of the uniforms that the waitresses in the bar at the hotel wear. I'll pay for it, of course. Can you see about getting one of those in my wife's size?"

That one took a little doing, and I ended up having to appeal to the vice president of the hotel before I could actually make that happen, but in the end, the guest got his uniform, though with a hefty price tag indeed.

"I have an idea for your suite as well," I said. "Could you scan a variety of pictures of the two of you throughout all your years together and send them to me?"

"Sure, no problem. I like where I think you may be going with that," he told me, but I said I wouldn't give him any more details about the surprise.

When the couple arrived, I had printed and framed the pictures all in matching frames, and they were hanging on the walls when they first entered the suite. The husband and wife were able to look at their entire thirty-plus years together as the violinist and accordionist began playing some of the couple's favorite songs (a list I'd had the guest compile and send me along with the pictures). As they walked through the room, the pictures told the story of their relationship; their marriage, a cross-country move, holidays, and other special times. All of those memories welcomed them to a weekend focused on celebrating their life together.

The wife adored the pictures and the roses, but when she saw the cocktail waitress uniform draped across the bed, the musicians said they heard a delighted giggle; then the door shut, and they didn't see the couple for the rest of the two hours while they played their concert.

The next day, the couple came down to thank me personally.

"You know, I'd been hoping to surprise my wife, but you went beyond that and surprised me too. We're both so touched by what you did."

"When you have a minute," the wife said, "we want you to come up to the suite and take a picture with us, surrounded by the other pictures."

To this day, I still have my copy of this picture to remind me of my own small part in their romantic story – one of many I have to tell.

•  •  •

Las Vegas is known for unplanned weddings, but one such wedding really sticks out in my mind. A couple approached us at the desk one day and told us that they'd like to get married... that same afternoon, when they returned from lunch in just a few hours! It was a spur-of-the-moment decision, but they wanted to have their wedding right there in our lobby.

While initially we felt a little bit of shock, we still had a few hours to prepare, and this was not our first time arranging for an impromptu wedding. What was a first was the story of this couple, though.

High-school sweethearts, this couple had eventually drifted apart. Life had separated them, and eventually they'd each fallen in love and married other people. In the backs of their minds, however, they'd each been wondering about the other all these years and deep inside, a flame still burned.

It just so happened that both of them had recently become widows, and as Fate would have it, they had run into each other unexpectedly here in Las Vegas, of all places.

Wanting to catch up, they'd agreed to get together for coffee, but it was no time at all before they realized that they were still very deeply in love.

I felt goose-bumps prickle my arms as I listened to their story. I was engrossed. It was better than any romance novel or movie I'd seen!

After hearing about how the couple had never stopped loving each other, every available person went to work preparing the wedding. We got the marriage license arranged (which doesn't take long in Vegas since there's no waiting period), filled the lobby with fresh white lilies, and even recruited one of the bartenders to play the piano.

When they arrived from their lunch, the couple's eyes glistened with tears. We were all touched by their story, and the testament to true love. And now after all that time and all those years, lifetimes lived apart, here they stood: hand in hand, finally saying the vows they'd thought they would say so long ago.

The couple still joins us every year for their anniversary, and we count ourselves blessed to have been witnesses to their wedding – and to how true love never really dies!

• • •

A lot of people want to propose to their partner in Vegas with a gambling theme. It's cute, but sometimes it can be tricky. One guest approached me and told me he wanted to propose to his girlfriend at a card table.

"I'm going to gamble on love," he told me. "Roll the dice and hope for the best."

Inwardly, I rolled my eyes, having heard every gambling pun a million times.

"This is going to be tricky," I told him. "Everything is strictly regulated by the gaming commission."

He asked about creating a fake game, but that was against the rules. Every game that takes place on the gambling floor has to be a live game. Eventually, we came up with the idea of having myself and a co-worker playing at the blackjack table where the couple was going to be. We arranged with the dealer and pit boss for the lucky lady to be presented with the engagement ring on her third winning hand.

When the couple arrived at the table, the boyfriend who had masterminded the ruse encouraged his girlfriend to place some bets. We started to make small talk, asking things like, "Where are you from?" and "What do you do?" She answered sweetly, all the while in the dark regarding her boyfriend's plans.

On her third winning hand, the dealer slapped a small black box on the top of her chips and slid the pile across.

She glanced around at us and then at her boyfriend. "What's with the box?"

The dealer shrugged while the boyfriend pretended to count his chips, but when she opened up the box, a quick, thrilled squeal escaped her lips. As she looked from the ring to her boyfriend, he slid off his stool and got down on one knee next to the table, where he officially proposed.

By that time, people at the other tables had noticed what was going on, and the gaming floor was the quietest I'd ever heard it as everyone held their breath, waiting for the girlfriend's answer. She finally said "yes," and the burst of applause brought the floor back to life just as one of our cocktail waitresses appeared with a chilled bottle of champagne. Everyone at the table toasted to the couple's happiness . . . but little did we know it was short-lived.

The couple found themselves in a situation that isn't that uncommon in Vegas. After all, it's a town where it's super-easy to get drunk, easy to get married, and then fairly easy to get divorced. In Las Vegas, it's not so much live-and-learn as it is live-and-forget.

And this was how I found my guest the next morning: hoping for a way to forget.

He was visibly upset; they'd celebrated their engagement a little too much and found themselves at a nearby chapel deciding to tie the knot immediately instead of waiting. Unfortunately, in that small space of time, she'd done something so unspeakable that he no longer had faith in the vows she'd taken.

Of course, he was crushed, and I did my best to console him as I scheduled transportation to the city courthouse. There, he would file an annulment. I also booked him a solitary ticket back home. This wasn't the first or last time that I transformed from concierge to marriage counselor, legal adviser and travel agent. As they say, everything's fair in love and war, but you'd better be ready for high stakes when you're gambling on love.

•   •   •

There I was, in the middle of one of our hotel rooms, tending to a bride-to-be. Not an unusual situation, except in this case, the bride-to-be was relatively calm yet completely naked.

She had come to me, a female concierge, for friendly fashion advice about her bridal wear, right down to her sexy, frilly lingerie. It was funny, actually. Here she was, her body covered in tattoos and her punk-rock pink hair. Judging from her appearance, one would think she had all the confidence in the world—especially since she was standing before me at the moment stark naked without any concern or embarrassment, yet she had sought out advice and affirmation. And I was flattered, but still felt strange and awkward.

I felt myself blush even redder (if that were possible), and she finally donned the wedding gown she'd been raving about. It turned out, however, to be too small. The back was a tangle of ribbons, completely losing the corseting effect it was supposed to convey. Instead of breaking down into tears, this Scandinavian bride-to-be turned this way and that in the mirror, calmly taking stock of the situation.

"I had a feeling it was not going to fit," she said, her accent heavy. "Too many Big Macs lately." She sighed. "That's just the way things go sometimes. But that's okay."

She bent down and grabbed the hem of the short skirt. Then I heard a nauseating rip.

"Oh, no!" I exclaimed, my hands flying to my mouth.

The bride looked up with a devilish grin and winked as she asked me to unzip her "just a little" in the back, allowing her to shimmy the sleeves a bit off the shoulders as she swept her pink hair to one side. In a matter of moments she had transformed herself into a modern day pin-up girl, complete with white fishnet gloves and edgy wedding dress to match.

"Amazing!" I said with a smile. "It's beautiful."

"I think so, yes," she agreed, admiring her handiwork in the mirror. "It's not the dress that makes the day anyway," she told me sagely.

Honestly, watching this Scandinavian woman go from naked to nuptial in a totally unique kind of way was one of the most powerful representations of love and commitment that I have ever witnessed. I truly appreciated the fact that she wasn't caught up in the details of the day, but understood the true meaning of this milestone.

We walked into the lobby to greet the groom, and my mouth dropped open in surprise when I saw him waiting for her in a one-of-a-kind neon green tuxedo.

"Congratulations, you two," I said, and I gave the bride a hug. "And rock on!"

# Very Unusual Requests

## Odd Numbers Only

By the time a concierge has
spent a year or two on the job,
he or she might think that
they've seen it all. They haven't!
No matter how strange a request
is, there's always one that will
top it. The following stories
will illustrate how even the
most seasoned concierge can be
blown away by guests' requests.

I'll admit it: there has been a time or two when I get an extremely unusual or outrageous request, and the thought goes through my mind—*I have heard it all now!* But then the next workday comes along, and yesterday's request is trumped by a newer, more unusual petition.

A gentleman guest called down to my desk one afternoon with what seemed at first like a straightforward request.

"I need your help," he explained. "I am going to be attending an American Indian barbecue, and I have been tasked with providing fuel for the fire."

I nodded, though he couldn't see me on the phone, and prepared to list off a few places where he could pick up a bag of charcoal. But then he continued his thought.

"It has to be authentic, though," he supplied.

I hesitated, unsure what he meant.

"Authentic?" I questioned.

"Meaning, I have to find a couple of bags of buffalo dumps. Do you have any idea where I can get something like that?"

Now, in case you didn't know, buffalo dumps – a.k.a. "meadow muffins" or "buffalo chips" – are pieces of dried bison dung. I'd heard of people who grew up on Texan farms using cow chips as Frisbees, so the idea wasn't completely foreign to me, but using them as barbecue fuel? Well, that was a new one.

"Let me see what I can do," I said, already consulting the Yellow Pages for nearby ranches and farms.

When I called the caretaker of a ranch about two hours' drive away, his first response was to laugh at my request.

"I can say I have never had anyone call and flat out ask for buffalo chips," he told me. And then he followed that with, "Hell, honey, if you make that two-hour drive to my ranch, you can have all the buffalo chips that you want."

I was ecstatic! Then I checked myself and recognized: I'd never been so excited over poop ever before in my life.

Within hours, I was sure that I was the source of many a laugh and memorable image for the rancher and his workers. For there I was, still in my professional attire—though I had taken off my formal captain-style jacket— roaming the buffalo fields for droppings. Just picture it: a concierge from a Vegas hotel in her black vest and pencil skirt, and three-inch heels. I tried to maintain my dignity and my balance while my heels sank into the grass as I shoveled bison poop into garbage bags.

The contrast of environments was stark. I was accustomed to being a part of the backdrop of a luxurious Vegas hotel, complete with gold trim and marbled floors, crystal chandeliers the size of houses lighting my every move. And here I was, surrounded by expansive fields and a random wandering buffalo chewing his cud, looking for the biggest and the best patties of excrement I could find . . . and being delighted at the booty I was hauling in.

Once I had filled two huge trash bags and piled them into the trunk of the car, I thanked the caretaker and asked him if the hotel owed him anything for the buffalo souvenirs.

"No way!" he replied with a big laugh. "I should be paying you for getting rid of the stuff, not to mention the sheer entertainment."

Hot and sweaty, I drove back to the Strip with the air conditioning on high, the smell of the buffalo ranch still in my nostrils.

When I got to the hotel, I took the two trash bags up to the guest's room. Finding he was out, I decided to have a little fun at his expense—he seemed like a good-natured guy, after all. So, I left the garbage bags in the corner of the room with a note that read: "Fuel for your fire. You can't say this hotel didn't do $#!T for you."

Later on that evening, the guest came by my desk, laughing as he approached.

"You know, I am simply amazed that you found the buffalo chips," he said. "But what really blew my mind was that not only did you find them, you went and got them for me—and you have a great sense of humor to boot! You have gone way beyond the call of duty here."

"Call of 'doody', eh?" I punned and winked at him as I laughed.

I later learned that he called my boss to sing the hotel's praises.

"Your people are unbelievable!" he exclaimed. "Who the heck would have ever thought that somebody would go so far out of their way to shovel poop for me?"

Who indeed?

•   •   •

Guests bring a lot of things with them to Vegas; their pets, their favorite pillows, their lucky charms. But the most unusual thing a guest ever brought with him to my hotel was an urn . . . full of his loved one's ashes.

"My partner Marty loved Vegas," he told me, and I watched his age-spotted hands slowly stroke the urn lovingly. "It's where we met and where he proposed. We came back every five years to celebrate our big anniversaries in Vegas. I think it was Marty's favorite place in the whole world."

I felt myself getting a little misty as I listened to the older man's stories. It was easy to see just how much Marty had meant to him.

"When Marty got sick, we started making plans. He knew he wanted to be cremated," the guest told me. "And he made me promise to take him to Vegas one last time."

"That's incredibly sweet," I told the guest, blinking away a tear as I glanced at the urn.

"I'd like to scatter his ashes on top of his favorite casino," the guest told me. "I promised him I'd do my best." He leaned forward across my desk. "Do you think you can help me make this happen?"

I was relatively certain I couldn't. After all, there were health laws and safety regulations that didn't permit anyone to throw *anything* from rooftops in Vegas, much less the cremated ashes of a person.

"I can't make any promises," I told the widower, "but I'll see if there's any way for us to grant Marty his last wish."

Just as I had suspected, none of my phone calls had a positive outcome.

I felt a stone in my stomach as I told the gentleman that in spite of all my best efforts, I couldn't find a way to make it happen.

Naturally, he was disappointed, and my heart dropped as I watched his face sink with the reality of my news. He nodded, thanked me for trying, and patted my hand before walking away from my desk, his head hanging low.

Later that evening I saw him leave the building. A few hours later, he returned, an exuberant smile on his face. I wondered what that smile was about.

"I found a way around it," he told me, "and I didn't have to sneak up to any rooftops."

"What did you do?" I whispered conspiratorially.

He told me he'd purchased a ticket for a popular roller coaster and taken the urn with him. When the roller coaster had got to the pinnacle, preparing to plunge downward, the guest had taken the lid off the urn, and by the time he'd stepped off the ride, the urn was empty.

At first I visualized all the people exiting the ride and brushing themselves off, a fine grey dust in their hair and on their shoulders. I could hear them wondering about how dusty the desert was without knowing what was really happening.

"I kept my promise!" the guest said to me, "and now Marty is exactly where he wanted to be: all along the Vegas Strip for all eternity."

• • •

Early on during my concierge career, I was working at a rundown Las Vegas property that has since been demolished. The carpets were faded, the lighting was poor, and the paint had cracked. Still, I did my best to provide five-star concierge assistance to my guests.

During the National Rodeo Finals held every year in December, one of the event's famous performers called me ahead of time with a most unusual request, even for Vegas.

"I need a room," he told me, "but I need something big enough so that I can bring my horse," he said.

I tried to explain our "No Pets" policy, but the rodeo star was adamant.

"You don't understand," he insisted. "My horse has to be with me, especially during nationals. Don't you have a villa or something like that, where there would be enough room for both of us?"

I will admit, I entertained the notion that perhaps this guy was pulling my leg, but when I began questioning him, the tone in his voice made me realize that indeed he was being very serious. So, I did what I do with any guest, no matter how outlandish the request: I decided I would do whatever I could to make this cowboy happy.

I went all the way up to the hotel chain president and was finally allowed to reserve a bungalow in the very back of the hotel complex for the rodeo star and his ride.

The weekend of the big rodeo finally arrived and our eccentric cowboy walked into the lobby. We had been preparing for days to accommodate a live animal, but when he arrived, our mouths all dropped to the floor in shock.

He was NOT accompanied by a real live horse, but a life-sized mock-up. He introduced him as his horse, and then told us how he always travelled with it.

"I'm too reluctant to store it elsewhere," he explained, "for fear it might get damaged, and I'd lose my best good-luck charm in the world. I've won five National Championships since I started traveling with my partner."

I was feeling a barrage of emotions all at once: embarrassment for my assumptions, relief that we had sidestepped trying to house a live horse, slight exasperation that this cowboy had led me on for so long and allowed me to fully believe in an honest-to-goodness horse he'd be bunking with. And underneath it all, there was an inkling of worry that my boss might possibly hog-tie me for putting him through all this!

To all intents and purposes, though, the cowboy hadn't lied: he did check in with an over-sized equestrian companion. I was just relieved that our kitchen never did have to deal with room service orders of buckets of oats and carrots.

• • •

I don't know about you, but when I think of someone celebrating his or her 80th birthday, I might picture a big family celebration, reliving the "good ol' days", and bringing in friends from far and wide to celebrate this major milestone. That was not the case, however, with a particular guest of mine back in the early 1990s.

The Strip then was not the Strip as we know it now.

One of our guests was turning eighty during his stay with us.

"I'm itching to do something I've never done before," he confided in me. "After all, I'm turning eighty, for crying out loud."

I suggested a few shows, or a friend who had a great ranch he could visit for horseback riding; I even suggested the most expensive restaurant in Vegas for his big day, but he shot down every suggestion with a curt shake of his aged, balding head.

Finally, he fixed his gaze on me. "Skydiving."

"What?" I wasn't sure if I'd heard him correctly.

"I want to go skydiving," he clarified.

It was the 1990s. There wasn't a ton of thrill rides then, much less a place for skydiving. My resources for this request at that particular time didn't even exist. I'd never had a guest get such a hare-brained idea as to go skydiving, especially not one who was preparing to turn eighty years old.

I finally tracked down a skydiving school in Boulder City, but they were quite reluctant to take a man of my guest's age skydiving.

"Look, he's requesting it to commemorate his eightieth birthday," I told them. "This is what he categorically has his mind set on doing."

Finally, they agreed, and though I had many scenarios in my head of how this could play out, I think that deep down inside, I didn't believe he'd actually go through with it.

But he did!

"What a rush!" he said as he came to tell me all about it. "You've never really lived until you've looked death right in the eye and told it 'Not now!'" were his words.

"I confess, I wondered if you would actually do it," I said.

"Think I'm a chicken, eh?" he challenged.

I shook my head defiantly. "Not at all. I was merely comparing you to myself. I wouldn't be able to actually do it when it came to jumping out of that plane."

He grinned and slammed his hand on my desk. "Well, now I want to go parasailing."

"You must be joking," I told him quite plainly. Then I saw that determined look in his eye that I'd seen previously, and I realized that he was, indeed, very serious.

"You can come along this time," he said.

I laughed and politely declined, but I set to work making the arrangements for him.

Again, he had a wonderful time, and again he told me about looking death in the face.

The following year, he joined us for his 81st birthday. When I saw his name on our reservation list, I began collecting a list of possible requests. I was actually quite nervous. Where would he take it this year? Bungee jumping? That seemed to be the new craze. Perhaps he'd want to drive a racecar.

Much to my relief, though, he arrived, greeted me with a kiss on the cheek, and told me he'd be keeping it simple this year.

"No death-defying acts?" I asked in mocked shock.

He patted my hand. "I've learned that at my age, every day is a death-defying act. This year, it's going to be a quiet celebration of eighty-one years. Just dinner and a show." Then he winked at me. "Plus, I don't want to show up the younger ones, now, do I?"

# It's Their Party

## Stacking the Chips

Some guests rely on concierges to plan fun parties, or come up with entertainment ideas, while others have created their own idea of fun and simply rely on the concierge to follow instructions. It's the latter of the two that can often send a concierge out on a wild goose chase, and make for some pretty funny and memorable times. As you'll see in the following stories, everyone has his/her own idea about what's fun and exciting.

I had only been a concierge for a few months when I got a call from a Canadian groom-to-be. He was a big fan of the CBS television reality show *The Amazing Race*, and he wanted to incorporate it into his wedding celebration.

"My bride and I are bringing seventy-nine of my closest friends and family members to Vegas for our wedding celebration," he explained. "What I'd like your help with is creating a city-wide scavenger hunt like *The Amazing Race* complete with challenges and tasks as well as items to find, et cetera."

"Sounds like fun," I said.

"One thing you should know is that my fiancée is a paraplegic and is confined to a wheelchair, but she has every intention of running the race with everyone else. I just want to make sure we incorporate a few tasks that will really allow her to excel."

I thought it was quite sweet that he wanted his bride to feel like an integral part of her team and to capitalize on her strengths.

"What else do you think I should know?" I asked as I started to jot down a few ideas that were already coming to mind.

"We're on a pretty strict budget," he replied. "In fact, we had to have a few fundraisers just to get enough money for everyone to go on the trip."

I wrote the word "budget" in big block letters on my brainstorming sheet as I told him I'd most certainly keep that in mind. Their trip was scheduled for a few months away, which granted me a little relief since planning this scavenger hunt/race would certainly take some time.

First on my list was to put together small backpacks for ten teams of eight people. These would be used during the race to hold things like disposable cameras, water bottles, and maps of the city and the Strip. I had the bright idea to call the local paper, thinking the story would make for a good 'special interest' piece for the locals, but surprisingly I didn't get very far there, and the newspaper nixed my idea.

With the help of an IT guy I knew, I used a special software package to map out the itinerary of the scavenger hunt, until we were thrown into a scavenger hunt of our own. The computer program crashed and we lost a big part of the customized information we had compiled thus far, so we had to go through tech support.

I made several stops some of the casinos so that the teams would have to find certain slot machines along their race. I knew this would get them out of the heat and provide a great challenge, as the Vegas casinos are veritable mazes so that gamblers have a hard time finding their way to the exit. I also knew that having them look for specific slot machines would be a great needle-in-a-haystack element to the race, as there are about two and a half slot machines per resident of Las Vegas. I had to stop myself from issuing a villainous laugh at this part of my plan.

There were a few times when I felt that my good intentions and hard work were not going to pay off, but finally, it was here. On a hot, steamy day at the end of August, the Canadian teams gathered for the first ever "Amazing Las Vegas Race." The excitement was palpable, and I began to feel my prior frustrations fading away. We set about laying the ground rules. The group – of which over half were senior citizens – could not use any cell phones, including Blackberries or other wireless devices—no GPS and no Smartphones. They could ask for help at hotels or other places, but they couldn't stop a stranger on the street to use their phone to access the internet. Also, for liability reasons, everyone agreed to limit themselves to taking public transportation.

I prepared myself for the moans and groans at the rules, but instead, someone piped up, "Where's Larry?"

Heads began to turn as people looked around for the missing person.

"We have to find him! He's our team leader," the bride said, laughing.

Someone left to check his room; another person left to check the casino next door, and yet another person headed to the bar, but they all returned with no sign of the bride's great uncle. I finally had to call security and get them involved as seventy-plus people milled around the lobby area waiting to get started.

Finally, in he walked with one of our security guards who'd found him wandering the sidewalks, and I had to explain all the rules again and restart the time. I wondered for a second if the team was considering canning their chosen leader, but they decided to stick it out with him, and soon, I blew the whistle for the race to begin.

At each stop on the Strip – the MGM Grand, New York, New York and so on – the teams were given clues, questions, or crazy tasks. One of the tasks was to dance like a Vegas showgirl with a willing stranger on Las Vegas Boulevard while someone documented it with the disposable camera. Teams also had to find a specific wedding chapel and stage an impromptu portrait of a wedding party comprised of team members. It was fun to think of these guests—many of whom were senior citizens— approaching locals and tourists alike, asking them for a dance, and then granting—and sometimes receiving—a peck on the cheek.

At one point, two of the teams colluded and stole another group's notebook, which was absolutely hilarious, but forced us to intercede and disqualify the teams for cheating. I thought it quite cheeky the way even the older people were determined to win at any cost, even if it meant they had to cheat a little!

In the end, I don't know who had more fun; me, setting it all up and listening to the tales of the race while helping to judge the winning team, or all the participants. It seemed that everyone involved, even the strangers enlisted to help, had a wonderful time, and it all culminated with a grand buffet at Main Street Station downtown.

The wedding rehearsal and the wedding itself were great highlights of the trip, but I think what made it especially memorable was the "Amazing Las Vegas Race", which I couldn't have done without the help of so many people within the city.

Even with all of their budget issues—which created a variety of sideline issues, causing us concierges to donate concierge certificates and tickets to cover the costs of their breakfasts—the entire group pooled their resources and granted me a generous tip.

I couldn't accept it though, especially once I had befriended the bride and learned her story. She'd been paralyzed from the waist down in a high school swimming accident. On her way to becoming a champion swimmer, her former hopes and dreams had been dashed within seconds. When I learned of their plans to travel to China for an expensive stem cell treatment, I donated my tip to help fund that trip, telling them it would mean a lot to me to be able to help in that way.

She and her husband, as well as some of the other Canadians in this group, became great friends of mine. They were the first of many guests with whom I would forge a lasting friendship, and the first of many guests I would count myself lucky to call "friends".

•  •  •

A very sweet couple was staying with us as they celebrated their twenty-fifth anniversary. One day the woman approached me.

"I want to do something special as a surprise for my husband, but I need your help," she said.

"Do you have something in mind already?" I asked.

She told me that she wanted to serenade him on the Strip, but she needed a piano in order to pull off this elaborate scene.

"Why the Strip?" I asked, to get a better idea of the thoughts behind her plan.

"I want it to be very public," she explained. "I want to be able to show him that I want everyone to know just how much I love him, how wonderful I think he is."

The idea was sweet and romantic, and I loved the sentiment behind it, but attempting to put a piano in the middle of the Vegas Strip would undoubtedly prove impossible.

"What about a piano bar?" I offered. "I know a few pianists who work in some great bars. I think we could convince them to hop off the stool long enough for you to do your thing."

Her mouth slid sideways as she thought about it. "The only thing is that it isn't extremely public. Not like being on the Strip would be. I'd like it to be more random and unplanned, and I would really like to do it in the afternoon, say around two o'clock."

Well, that cut out the piano bars; none of them opened until early evening.

I asked her to give me a little time to think it through and ask some of my colleagues for some ideas, and she agreed to come back within a few hours' time to see how far I'd gotten. When a hotel guest entered the door laden with shopping bags, the iconic red silver "N" on a slate gray backing caught my eye.

"Doesn't Nordstrom's have in-store pianists?" I asked a fellow concierge suddenly.

"I think so. Isn't that, like, their 'thing'?"

I googled the number and picked up the phone to dial. When I got the manager on the phone, I asked the question again.

"We do have a pianist; however, he isn't 'in-house' anymore really. Since we're in the mall, we have limited store space, and now he plays just outside our entrance in the mall space."

How much more public could you get at two in the afternoon? I explained the situation and my guest's request, and the manager quickly agreed to conspire to help and put me in touch with the pianist. Thankfully, he too was a hopeless romantic. He thought the idea was great and became just as excited about it as I was.

I told my guest, and together we called the pianist back and set things in motion.

The next day, the wife sent her husband on an errand to Nordstrom's at the mall. We provided him transportation service, but only after I had instructed the driver to take a more scenic route in order to buy us a little time. The wife, in the meantime, left shortly after her husband in a cab I'd called for her, and arrived with extra time to warm herself up on the keyboard.

As if planned by the Divine, the mall was busier than usual with end-of-season sales happening in all the stores. As shoppers strolled by and others hung around to people-watch, the sound of the piano welcomed them on the second floor, right outside the entrance to the cooperating store. The wife played a few pieces while she kept her eye out for her husband, and when she saw him approaching the piano and the store entrance, she began playing "their song".

"Unforgettable," she sang, "That's what you are ... Unforgettable, though near or far ..."

The sound of her voice stopped her husband in his tracks, and he laughed first at the fact that he had been fooled, but as his wife sang to him, he told me later, the tears sprang to his eyes as the realization of what she was doing began to set in.

Then, to the wife's surprise and to the onlookers' delight, the husband sat down beside her on the piano bench and joined in with her to sing the chorus and the final verse, punctuating the ending with the sweetest of kisses. Everyone had stopped strolling and people-watching as their attention was riveted to the couple, and when the song ended with the joining of their lips, the entire mall broke into applause and cat-calls.

In an inspired and impassioned moment, the husband slid from his place on the piano bench onto one knee on the floor.

"You have been my partner, my lover, my best friend for twenty-five years," he said in a loud, strong voice. "And I want at least twenty-five more with you. You've made me the happiest man on earth, and I'd love it if you'd agree to re-marry me again on our anniversary. I want to recommit my life and happiness to you. What do you say? Want to renew our vows tonight?"

Her eyes glistening with tears and her cheeks blushed red with emotion, the wife emphatically nodded her head before her voice finally spoke the "Yes" that her husband and the onlookers were so eagerly awaiting.

"So here we are needing your help again," the wife said to me as she looked lovingly at her husband. "We're going to one of the wedding chapels on the Strip, but we'd really like a limousine to take us there and then to dinner afterward."

"That is easily arranged," I told them. "Just let me know what time you'd like them to arrive."

But I had one trick up my own sleeve for the couple who had surprised each other. Earlier during their stay, I had stopped in the lobby to make small talk with some of the guests. The husband had been there reading a book while his wife did some shopping. We got to talking, and I'd learned that he was passionate about two things in his life: his wife and antique cars.

"I've even had a few through the years," he told me, and joked about how great it was that his wife allowed him such a time-consuming and often expensive pastime. "She even goes to all these classic car shows with me. I know it's not her favorite thing—though she's becoming quite an expert on the subject—but she does it because she knows how much I enjoy it," he said.

"And most likely because she enjoys being with you," I concluded, to which he nodded in agreement.

When the couple walked away after asking about the limousine, something clicked in my mind. I had met a local man who drove a beautiful, gleaming 1953 Cadillac Eldorado convertible—mint condition. He was often paid to chauffeur people to special events such as proms, and would sometimes drive queens in various parades. Thinking of my special couple, I called him up to ask if he'd be willing to drive my guests to their renewal ceremony and to dinner afterward.

He was thrilled to be invited to play a part in such a sweet scheme and his beautiful Cadillac shone in all the lights. The driver (dressed in a tuxedo) got out and came around to open the door for them. They were so impressed and touched at this little detail I'd surprised them with.

The most wonderful thing about it all was that the driver had had the Cadillac for exactly twenty-five years, so he was celebrating an anniversary of sorts himself. What a perfect way for this sweet couple to celebrate their twenty-five years together, and I was happy that I had been able to help them commemorate the experience.

•　•　•

I will never forget the Playboy Golf Tournament. I'd only been working at the host hotel for about two weeks when the time for the tournament came around. It was a great golf competition, but as the host hotel, we also had many other events planned for the guests gathering for the event.

Along with one-hundred-and-fifty gentlemen who arrived for the tournament, there were the Playboy Bunnies and other Playmates, the Playboy Girls of Golf, as well as various models from all over the world.

Once we had all of the guests checked in and they were all settling into their accommodations, our Director of Casino Services announced that we were going to have a toga party. I looked at the clock. It was already four in the afternoon, and I knew that all of the girls—and most likely the other guests—were going to be in need of toga costumes. We sent out employees, but it was early November. Halloween had come and gone and taken all of its togas with it. In fact, there was only one or two available.

So, we began to brainstorm. Finally, one of the girls from housekeeping told us of a long-abandoned stash of older sheets they no longer used, and we all leapt from our desks and ran to the closet. Finding the stack of sheets satisfactory, we decided we'd simply create our own customized toga outfits.

Except that it wasn't as simple as one might think.

Keep in mind that most of the people who were helping had no idea how to sew or make costumes. On top of that, we were faced with the task of making those customized togas for more than a hundred guests! Trust me, we had our work cut out for us, so to speak.

Luckily, I had some experience in the costume industry, so I knew enough to create passable costumes, but there was no way I could outfit all of those girls by myself. So, I recruited help from some of the hotel managers and directors. We grabbed buttons, ropes, curtain tie-backs, and any decorative items we could find and armed ourselves with hot glue, pins, needles and thread, and even staples!

All of this took place on a Friday evening, so we had our regular and weekend guests there in addition to our Playboy Bunnies and the golf crew. The guests walking through the black-and-white marbled lobby, watching us throwing sheets over these girls and pinning them into various drapes, must have thought it was hilarious. Here were all these older hotel managers and directors in three-piece suits and ties running around stapling up these half-naked Playboy Bunnies – or on their hands and knees sewing and pinning these costumes on! All in all, we created one-hundred-and-twenty toga costumes in just over an hour. The girls had a great time, and it is still rumored to be one of the best events the casino has ever hosted, with some Playboy guests marveling that it was a party to rival many of the parties given at the Playboy Mansion by Hugh Hefner himself.

• • •

Seeing impersonators or getting an opportunity to hang out with a look-a-like is another charm in Las Vegas. One of my guests was going to be celebrating her eightieth birthday during her stay.

Her family wanted to surprise her with something really special, and they told me that she was a huge fan of Frank Sinatra. Since I know several impersonators, I knew exactly how to help this family make this lady's birthday quite memorable . . . and get the pictures to commemorate it.

I made reservations for the guest and her family at one of the finest restaurants in Vegas, and during her meal, the woman got a singing telegram. The person delivering the telegram was the Frank Sinatra impersonator, but he wasn't just "any" Frank Sinatra impersonator. He was the absolute best! He not only looked like Frank Sinatra, but he could sing like him, unlike several impersonators who rely on lip-synching. He was an absolute crooner.

When he arrived at her table and began singing "Happy Birthday", the woman was as shocked as the family, for I hadn't told them to expect him. They bombarded me with their thanks when they returned that night, but I was able to simply smile, shrug, and tell them, "It's what we do here in Vegas."

"Well, you couldn't have done better," the birthday girl told me. "If I didn't know better, I would have sworn Old Blue Eyes had come back from the grave when I saw and heard that guy sing to me."

And I grinned knowing that, in a way, a dream had come true that night.

• • •

Probably the most popular impersonators in Vegas are the Elvis impersonators. It isn't odd to get a request for an Elvis impersonator to be at the wedding chapel for the ceremony, either. But I had a certain couple one year whose Elvis requests went beyond anything I had ever heard.

The couple had made it clear that they wanted to do the whole "Viva Las Vegas" theme for their wedding, complete with an Elvis impersonator and Elvis-themed chapel for the ceremony.

"This will be easy," I remember telling them. And when I found out it was going to be a small ceremony—only ten to twelve guests—I relaxed.

They arrived, and I welcomed them to their wedding weekend. I explained to them all the arrangements that had been made, and they settled into their suite. The next day—the day of the wedding—they sprang their final request upon me:

"We got to thinking, and we wanted something that would really set our ceremony apart from the other Elvis-themed weddings that happen in Vegas," the husband-to-be began. "So, what we decided is this: we want the wedding party—our guests coming that weekend—to be in Elvis costumes, too, for the ceremony."

I felt my relaxation coming to a screeching halt. Renting a few Elvis costumes would have been easy, but I wasn't sure if I could find that many in just a few hours.

Within minutes after being told, I was running all over Las Vegas, cleaning out Elvis costumes from every party shop and costume boutique I could find. While the women who were dressing up were a bit pickier about the type of costume they wore, we were able to settle any disputes relatively easily with some compromising, and in the end, everyone looked really great! The ceremony was a great combination of sweetness and hilarity, and I still keep a photo of the "Elvis wedding audience" on my desk.

And speaking of Elvis, I remember a guest calling me one day to tell me that he wanted to book our hotel to celebrate his mother's birthday. Family would be gathering from many different states, and they wanted to do something very special. The guest's mother would be turning eighty (obviously a birthday that brings many adults out to Vegas), and she absolutely adored Elvis. So, the guest wanted to do something related to Elvis.

Brainstorming aloud, I gave him a few suggestions. "We could always get an impersonator to sing to her; that's a popular request. Or maybe we could even have Elvis jump out of a birthday cake."

"Let's go bigger," he said excitedly. "I'd love to find an Elvis impersonator who will take her for a ride on Las Vegas Boulevard on a Harley-Davidson," he said. "She's always wanted to do that."

When a guest has specific ideas, it can be great, or it can be challenging. Sometimes, it's heartbreaking to tell a guest that the specific vision he or she has is simply impossible, but if it's all do-able, the specifics often make my job a little easier.

"Oh my," I replied, chuckling at the visual I was already getting of this guest's idea. "Well, I'll definitely see what I can do," I told him, while I must confess, I was thinking, *I hope you checked this out with Mom first!*

It was actually easier to find a motorcycle-riding Elvis impersonator than I first thought, and I got everything set up. On the big day, I can still remember the woman's face when she came outside and saw Elvis Presley sitting on a Harley, gesturing for her to join him. She was so precious and such a sweet lady! I did have a fleeting moment when I wondered about her health and if her heart was in good condition.

Still, her family helped get her situated on the bike and strapped a helmet on her. She held on tightly to Elvis, and off they went! I was quite nervous at that point, feeling responsible for her safety and her health; I was afraid she might be upset or shaken up when they got back. To my surprise, the very moment they returned, the woman took off the helmet, checked in with her family, and let a devious smile spread over her face.

"Let's go again!" she said.

• • •

It's a common theme: when people come to Las Vegas to celebrate, they have every intention of doing it bigger, better, and more elaborate than ever before. That was exactly what one husband—Tom—had in mind for his wife, Stacy.

Tom and Stacy lived just outside Las Vegas, and he called me one day telling me about his plan to surprise his wife for Valentine's Day, which happened to be on a weekend. He'd already booked the hotel months in advance, but as the date was coming up, he wanted to enlist my help to do something very special for his wife; something outside the box.

"Valentine's in Vegas sounds incredibly special," I encouraged, but then told him that I would do my best to make it even more memorable for the two of them.

He and I chatted about it for a while, and I asked him to tell me their story so that I could generate some ideas tailored to them. During the conversation, it came out that she loved balloons – had always loved them, even as a child – and he'd incorporated balloons into the milestones of their life. He had even proposed in a hot-air balloon, and after they were married, he had the honeymoon suite loaded with balloons for their first night as husband and wife.

"Let's start there," I suggested. "How many would you want? We could fill the outer room of your suite."

"Eight hundred," was the answer that came without hesitation.

My eyes bugged out, and I'm sure my mouth dropped open, but I began thinking through how to get eight hundred balloons into their suite and how to time it all to surprise his wife.

We also came up with a plan for her day, and when Valentine's morning arrived, I called his wife at their house to tell her that a car would be picking her up in an hour.

"I didn't order a car," she replied, and then I heard her ask her husband about a car that was ordered. He told her to just go with it, and so she thanked me and hung up the phone.

From miles away, I imagined the look on her face when she went out to find a limousine parked in her driveway. I could almost see the confusion furrowing her brow as she crawled in, but an envelope with her name was waiting for her on the seat, and I knew that would explain that she was being taken to her favorite restaurant for a complementary private lunch.

When she arrived at the restaurant, she was told that her meal had been paid for by an admirer. She ordered her favorite food and wine and ate a leisurely lunch, something she never got to do as an elementary school teacher who ate with kindergarteners every day of her life.

After lunch, she was driven back home in the limo, where Tom had left her another note telling her to pack an overnight bag. The limousine driver then delivered her directly to our hotel spa, where she got the royal treatment.

After her spa session, I personally escorted her to the suite her husband had already checked into secretly. We stepped into the main room, and with the high ceilings, I had to admit that the eight hundred balloons created quite a dramatic effect. Stacy laughed in utter joy at the sight. I apprised her that a new dress was waiting for her in the bedroom closet, and a car would be waiting to take her to a special dinner. I knew there was a lot of helium in the room, but from what I could tell, Stacy was already walking on air.

"Tom will meet you there," I said to her, and for a second, I think I was almost as excited as she was at how beautifully the plan had been working.

The restaurant Tom had chosen was also where he and his wife had first met, and it was already obvious that Stacy was not only flattered but also thrilled by all the mystery and surprise. It was a very beautiful Valentine's Day that ended with chocolate-covered strawberries, chilled champagne, and fresh roses in their bedroom.

I loved the fact that after all their years of marriage, the husband still knew how to be romantic, but I couldn't help wondering how in the world he'd top that Valentine's Day the following year!

# Naughty Bits

## Serious Steam

One of the funniest things about people in Las Vegas is that they're less inhibited. They come to Vegas to have an amazing time and when they arrive, their insecurities seem to go out of the door! Sometimes, they try to get the concierge to help them get certain items, or do certain things. This can often be fun and hilarious, but sometimes, a concierge has to lay down the law. As you'll see from the following stories, things can really get steamy in Las Vegas.

A bachelorette party notified me that they wanted to celebrate in a special way. Rather than going to the strip club to get an eyeful of the male dancers, this group of twelve had decided on a new spin: they wanted to actually get on stage and dance for their friend – no holds barred! Unfortunately (or fortunately, perhaps), the strip clubs in Las Vegas have very strict rules and regulations when it comes to their dancers, and there is red tape for miles.

I pulled my lips back in a grimace. "I appreciate your unique style," I told them, "but I seriously doubt I can make this happen for you."

Cindy, the girl who seemed to have taken on the leadership role, shook her head. "I believe in you," she said to me. "There must be one strip club where we can give it a try."

I looked at them, their eyes pleading with me.

I sighed. "Let me make some calls. I will see what happens, but I'm afraid the outlook isn't too hopeful. There are a lot more regulations regarding these clubs and their dancers than one could imagine."

Cindy smiled and patted my hand. "Just let us know what you find out."

Without much confidence, I called around to nearly every strip club in Vegas. I explained to them the plan the women had concocted and asked if it would be possible.

One after another turned me down. A few even laughed at me.

"We want nothing to do with that," one manager even said to me. "Do you even know what you're asking?"

Finally, I called a good friend of mine, who was also the owner of a smaller nightclub just off the Strip.

"I have to admit I'm a little intrigued," he told me. "However, there are conditions."

I felt some hope rise within me. "Just tell me what they are. I have a feeling these girls will go to almost any lengths to make this happen for their friend."

"The condition for your ladies to dance is that they have to audition just like any other dancer. We can't guarantee they'll be given the green light even after the audition, but if they do make it, they can only spend two songs on stage."

My small flame of hope waned to a bit of an ember. With no experience of dancing, I had a feeling these girls were in for disappointment. I tried to adopt the confidence the girls had in me.

I called up to Cindy's room and gave her the news. She sounded a little let-down, but I could tell she wasn't going to give up her plan so easily.

"Well, we'll just have to practice a bit," she told me resolutely.

"Wait a second," I uttered, "I just got a great idea." And after calling a few places, we booked a pole dancing class at a great place on the Strip for the entire bachelorette party.

The rules at the club, however, only allowed six girls to go on stage, so the women had to make a decision: who would be the lucky six to gift their friend with a strip-tease while the others developed and executed a story to get the bride-to-be to the club?

On the big night, even I was nervous and excited for the girls to pull off their big prank. At the very last minute, two of the girls chickened out, their nerves getting the best of them. Cindy and the other three, however, strutted out onto the stage with enough confidence for the entire crew.

The bachelorette was stunned almost to the state of disbelief, especially when they pulled her onto the stage, embarrassed and giggling, tied her to the chair and danced to their two songs. The non-dancers shoved dollar bills towards the bachelorette so that she could show her gratitude, and the crowd hooted and hollered.

I had to give them props for the courage and self-confidence it took them to pull that off. I can honestly say I've never had another bachelor or bachelorette party attempt anything quite as wild. As for my friend who owned the club, he called me soon after with a new proposition.

"If you have requests like that in the future, please let me know. We took in more money during the bachelorette party's dance than we did with our professionals all night long!"

I was happy to give the girls that message when they were checking out.

"I guess if you ever decide on a new career, you'll have a place to start," I teased. I had to do a double-take, however, when I realized that two in the party were wearing beaks and chicken feathers. "What gives?" I asked.

Cindy jerked her head towards the ladies in feathers. "They chickened out, so now they pay the price."

I laughed. I'd seen many men who were serious about their pranks, their golf or their boxing matches, but I'd never seen this level of penalty among any of those groups. These women were passionate and creative and took their bonds very seriously. Regardless, I think the bride-to-be left Las Vegas understanding just how far her friends were willing to go for her . . . and it was probably farther than she'd ever imagined!

• • •

Birthdays are common celebrations among our guests. I had a guest coming to Vegas to celebrate her fiftieth birthday, and she wanted to make it really special. She waltzed over to my desk and slapped down five crisp one-hundred-dollar bills.

"I want you to go on a shopping spree for me," she said.

"Sounds fun!" I told her, already thinking of the fun I could have at the trendy boutique shops I loved to frequent.

"Spend every bit of it, and spend it all in one place," she told me.

"Really?"

"Yes: the adult superstore." She winked at me and then started giggling. Before I could ask any questions, she waved and was out the door.

*Oh my god*, I thought. *You can buy a lot of stuff at an adult store for five-hundred dollars!*

I have to admit, I didn't have a lot of experience at the adult store, and I was trying to determine what I should buy for her: maybe some lotions, edible panties, chocolate novelties, a vibrator? But I would still have plenty of money left over.

I decided to ask for some advice, so I went to my friend who was working the desk.

"I just got an interesting assignment," I said, and then I told her.

"I love that lady!" she said. "She's one of my favorite guests ever! I would love that assignment." Then she laughed. "But it's great that you have to do it! Hilarious!"

"What's hilarious?" another colleague asked as he passed by, and my friend filled him in. Much to my chagrin, he began laughing.

"What's so funny?"

"I have to admit, I'd like to see you on a big shopping spree at the adult store. That *would* be hilarious."

"You guys are so perverted," I joked with my fellow staff members. Suddenly, I had a thought. "I think if you're so interested in it, *you* should do the shopping!"

Not surprisingly, they jumped at the opportunity. Their faces shone with the anticipation of kids on Christmas morning. I knew I had done the best thing: saved myself from an embarrassing shopping expedition and given them the opportunity to go shopping for adult toys.

A few hours later, I was returning to the hotel after running a few other errands. When I got back to my desk, I found its entire surface was covered in various phalluses that were whirling, vibrating, and rotating. There was an assortment of flavored lotions and oils, not to mention a stack of videos with ample-bosomed women in a range of intriguing positions. There were even some items on my desk that I couldn't readily identify!

I was standing there looking at the mini-sex shop that was my desk when my boss walked into the office. Accustomed to the ways of Vegas, my easy-going boss took a long look at my desk, glanced back up at me and said, "What happens at the concierge desk stays at the concierge desk." With his hands in the air, he walked out of my office, smiling, never even asking about the objects or why they were on my desk! Gathering them all up, my colleagues and I decorated the woman's room with all of the paraphernalia her money had bought. It was fun to think of creative ways to display them; almost like leaving little treasures all over her room for her to find.

If I told you she was *thrilled* with the outcome, would you really be surprised?

• • •

A few years ago, we had a particularly memorable bachelorette party at our hotel with a huge lineup of bridesmaids with a lot of plans and a tight schedule. As I was scrambling around to make sure everything was going off without a hitch, a bridesmaid came down to my desk carrying a rather large, nondescript box.

"Excuse me," she said to me.

"Yes? Is there something I can help you with?" I asked.

She burst into giggles and her face reddened. "Yes," she was finally able to say.

Her laughter was contagious, and soon I was joining her and giggling too. She handed me the box.

"Can you unpack the item in here, blow it up, and bring it upstairs to the suite? We want to put it in the bachelorette's room for the night."

"No problem," I told her, already thinking about trying to squeeze this new task onto my to-do list, but I was accustomed to that type of thing. I took the item out and, seeing the size, I quickly realized there was no way I was going to be able to blow it up by myself, so I recruited a couple of guys from maintenance to help inflate it.

They were happy to oblige, but as they were blowing it up and the item was taking shape, I think they began to resent their helpfulness. I left them to expel their hot air while I took care of a few phone calls and memos, checking on some of the plans for the bachelorette party. I was so busy and "in the zone" that I wasn't paying any attention to the maintenance workers as they were finishing up their task for me.

Finally, one of them cleared his throat, and I glanced up to see him standing next to an eight-foot penis. He had turned only slightly red, but I burst into a cackle.

"It's all yours," he said, pushing it toward me.

"I have to carry this thing all the way up to the Penthouse Suite?" I asked.

"Better you than me," he said with a laugh, and he and his partner turned and high-tailed it out of there.

I squared my shoulders and lifted my head, throwing the eight-foot appendage over my shoulder as if I did this type of thing every day of my life. Only a few guests whispered and pointed. It's pretty safe to say they all got the last laugh.

●　●　●

I was a few weeks into my first Las Vegas concierge job when I got a rather unusual call from one of the penthouse suites.

"Could you send up some ladies?" the man asked. "Nothing illegal, of course. We just need some ladies to make our party more interesting."

I cleared my throat and then launched into the spiel I'd been instructed to give: "I'm sorry I can't help you sir; that is against hotel policy, regardless of how mild or tame your activity may be."

"Even if I promised?" he asked. "Isn't there something I could sign, perhaps, to ensure I wouldn't violate any hotel policy?"

"I'm sorry. I still can't help you. Thank you for understanding."

I hung up, relieved that it had gone as smoothly as possible. A few minutes later, I got a call from the same man.

"I'd like to speak to a male concierge, please," the man insisted.

"I'm sorry, sir. I'm the only concierge on duty right now. There will be a male concierge back in two hours or so, but I'm happy to assist you with whatever you need."

"No. No offense," he said. "It has to be a man. Don't you have someone there I can talk to?"

The only staff member on call at that time who fit the bill was my manager. I felt bad about having to bother him, but the guest was insistent.

When I summoned my manager, somewhat apologetically, he rolled his eyes. "I would be willing to bet this call has something to do with female companionship," he predicted.

*But I just told him about our policy*, I thought. Sure enough, the manager was soon informing the guest again that there was nothing he could do.

My manager looked at me. "Don't know why he couldn't ask you to help him. You could turn him down just as easily as I could have," he joked.

"He called down here earlier, and I did turn him down," I provided. "Maybe he just thought he could appeal to you as a man."

My manager laughed before walking away from my desk. I got busy with other things, but apparently my guest couldn't get his problem off his mind. He also must have been a believer in the theory that everything is possible if you throw enough money around. Believe it or not, he called back a few minutes later to lay out his request in greater detail.

"I'll pay you $1,000 for each woman you can get up here, and I'll pay the women $1,000 each as well. I just want them to hang out, maybe take their tops off."

Frankly, I was beginning to feel a bit exasperated with the whole thing.

"Sir, I am very sorry. I don't like telling my guests 'no', but do you know what I like less? Being jobless. There's just no way I can help you. Even if I wanted to help, I'm pretty new in town; I don't even know six girls in Vegas yet that I could call for you."

He sighed. "Thanks anyway."

About an hour later, I saw a few beautiful girls making their way to the bank of hotel elevators. A few moments later, there were a few more. They headed to the elevators and disappeared, only to return a few hours later leaving the hotel together, as if they were friends.

I have no idea where the man found these women, but I know they were well paid.

"Are you kidding me?" one of my friends asked when I told her about the man's request. "I would have totally gone and spent a few hours hanging out at a party for $1,000."

I laughed and told her, "And then you'd have to loan it to me because I'd have been out of a job!"

•　　•　　•

Occasionally, Las Vegas concierges have to learn the hard way. I was the new kid on the block when a guest approached me, giggling almost uncontrollably.

"I'd love to help you if I can," I said to the guest.

Finally, she took a deep breath and said in a quick rush, "Can you help me find the nearest chicken ranch?"

I smiled and told her that I was new to the area, but I would be glad to do some research and let her know what I found.

She thanked me and left, laughing quite loudly. I did a Google search locally for "chicken ranch" but came up with nothing.

When I went into the back room, a few of my colleagues were there. A part of me wanted to ask them about local chicken ranches, but I was afraid I would embarrass myself for not figuring out such a simple request on my own. I smiled at the group, rolling my eyes at myself inwardly, and resumed my research, still turning up with nothing.

After a few minutes of non-productive searching, I laid my head in my hands in frustration.

"What's wrong?" one of my colleagues asked when he noticed me. "You've been frowning at that computer for quite some time."

"It's just something a guest asked me to find for her," I replied.

"What is it?"

"She asked where the nearest chicken ranch was. Do you know about any?"

He looked at me for a moment and then burst out laughing.

"What?" I asked innocently.

It took him a minute to catch his breath, during which I flashed back to the woman's hilarity as she asked me to find one for her. It slowly began to dawn on me that these two both shared the humor in the situation that I couldn't quite grasp.

"A chicken ranch is a brothel... a whore house," he finally said.

"What?!" My eyes widened, and I could feel my cheeks slowly turning red with the realization.

"It's vernacular for a whore house," he said again. "And just for the record, we can't help the guests look for those."

I covered my face, unable to look at him anymore. Already I was wondering how I would explain to the woman that I couldn't help her find her requested chicken ranch. After all, I was brand new to the job.

"Make sure you tell the guest that it's against hotel policy," my colleague said.

"I don't know if I can look her in the eye," I said.

"Just remember: this is probably the first of several times you're going to get this request. After all, you're in Vegas. And it's best to learn the lingo so you know what guests are really seeking."

I knew he was right, but it didn't make it any easier for me to anticipate the conversation with the woman. I called her room, feeling that I'd rather tell her the news over the phone than face to face. Thankfully, she answered, and I informed her that I couldn't help her find what she was looking for as it was against our policy to give out that sort of information.

She took it well, but my colleagues teased me for months, sometimes asking if I'd like to take a little trip to the nearest chicken ranch or if I'd like a ranch chicken sandwich for lunch, anything that alluded to the euphemism.

"It's a shame you had to lose your innocence like that," my colleague said to me one day.

Eventually I just shrugged and said, "I guess it was bound to happen in this town sooner or later!"

• • •

We had a high-betting guest named Dave who frequented our hotel quite a bit. During one of his stays, a bellman approached me. I could tell from his smirk and the extra hop in his step that he had something up his sleeve, and I wondered how it would pan out for me.

"Dave sent me with a request," he told me.

"From the look on your face, it's a doozy," I remarked.

"Well, it's actually his girlfriend, or his girlfriend of the day," he winked, "who has the request."

"Okay," I said waiting for him to deliver.

"I must say, I've never had a request like this. I'll be interested to know if you have."

I could tell he was enjoying building the suspense, but it was holding me up, and I had a lot to get done that day, so I motioned for him to issue the request.

"It seems that she needs a" – he gestured a little, fingers pointing toward his chest – "a ring."

I cocked my head to the side. "A ring?" I asked.

The bellman let out a shot of laughter, looked around, and then leaned in toward me. "A nipple ring!" he whispered.

My first thought was, *You've got to be kidding me!* My second thought was, *Find them and take care of this pronto without drawing a lot of attention to the issue.*

"Where are they now?" I asked the bellman.

"Pool," he replied.

So I strode out of the air-conditioned lobby and headed in that direction, trying very hard to look like I handled this sort of problem all the time. The 112-degree weather felt more like 150, and by the time I'd reached the group, bullets of sweat were forming under my black skirt and suit jacket. As I arrived at the cabana, a young girl came bouncing up to me.

"Hi. I'm Vanessa. Listen, thanks so much. I'm in trouble." Then – without any hesitation or reservation at all – she yanked her top off, revealing both of her large breasts. "My piercing came out," Vanessa explained.

My mouth must have dropped to the concrete, though I was trying to keep the shock from registering on my face. She gave me a pitiful look, most likely because my eyeballs were about to pop out of their sockets.

"I think the ball fell off," she continued, still topless, "and it won't stay in."

I nodded slowly and maintained careful eye contact. "Okay." I began thinking through everything. I knew a little bit about piercings, so I asked what gauge ring she needed, hoping to quickly make my escape.

"I don't know." She frowned, and then suddenly, she pulled the piercing out of her nipple and thrust it towards me. "Here. Maybe you can tell me."

Pulling out the tiny notebook I kept in my pocket, I smiled, and held it out to her. She placed the little ring on the notebook, tied her bikini top back on, and bounced back to the group to enjoy the pool some more. With a sigh, I went off to find the girl a new nipple ring. I found myself at a tattoo and piercing shop, her nipple ring in a small baggie, asking about one exactly like it as a replacement. About thirty minutes later, I returned victorious, brandishing a tiny plastic bag with a brand new nipple ring inside. When Vanessa saw us approaching, she grinned warmly.

After handing over the jewelry, Vanessa hugged me, the smell of coconut oil lingering even after she'd left me. I waved and told them I was glad to help, but Vanessa dropped her top again, calling me back.

"Can you help me put it back in?" she asked. "It's kinda hard to see."

Inside, I was thinking, *Why can't Dave, your boyfriend, help you with that?* Aloud and politely, I said, "I'm afraid I can't do that... legal purposes, you know. I would be happy to take you to a professional if you need one."

She was already shaking her head. "Nah, but maybe you have a pair of pliers?"

I felt my body involuntarily wince. "I'm afraid not. We would be liable for any damages." My eyes darted from side to side, taking in the crowd of people surrounding us, enjoying the heat and the pool, and I was afraid some might catch a view of Vanessa they would rather enjoy.

By this time, I didn't think I could become any more uncomfortable with both the topic we were discussing and the sweltering heat. Again, I said my goodbyes and felt fine about leaving Vanessa with the task of figuring out how to jam the nipple ring into her flesh by herself. For some reason, however, she leaned forward a few inches and said, "So, I was thinking of getting this awesome genital piercing..."

I didn't think it could get hotter or more claustrophobic, but suddenly it did, and I was feeling faint and clammy. I mumbled something about having work to do, and quickly exited, hoping that if she did go through with a new piercing, I wouldn't be expected to help replace that ring . . . ever.

# Funny: Ha Ha!

## What are the Odds?

Perhaps one of the greatest challenges is keeping it together for guests when all you want to do is giggle until you cry. There are many times when a guest will do or say something very hilarious, but a concierge wouldn't dare laugh at someone they were serving. Of course, there are times when the guests and the concierge share a chuckle, but those times when a concierge shouldn't laugh can often be the funniest!

At one point early in my career as a concierge, I was working the overnight shift at a small Las Vegas boutique hotel where they wanted a concierge on duty at all hours. It was just myself and a desk clerk that evening, which was a stroke of luck for the gentleman who appeared later on.

It was around two in the morning when we heard a loud male voice coming from the direction of the elevators.

"Help! Can someone please help me?"

The voice was quite loud and urgent, which prompted both my colleague and me to share the same thought: call security!

Within seconds of picking up the walkie talkie, however, a very wrinkled and very naked older man walked into the main lobby area. His hands were covering his privates, and he had a sheepish look on his reddened face.

Quickly, I grabbed a couple of pillows from the lobby couch and sandwiched his body between them. His sheepish look broke as he shot me a glance of relief for a second as he gladly accepted the temporary cover.

"Sir, what happened?" I asked, trying to figure out what in the world would have brought this man to the lobby at two a.m. without a single stitch of clothing.

"Obviously he got locked out of his room," the desk manager said. "Can I give you another keycard?" he asked the old man.

The man shook his head. "My key is in my room."

"Well, I'll walk you back and let you in," I suggested.

"I don't know if that's such a good idea," the gentleman faltered.

"Sir, please. We just want to help you. What's the matter?" I heard myself asking what sounded like a ridiculous question. Obviously, the matter was that he was naked and locked out of his room, and for some reason he was a bit hesitant to return. I rephrased my query. "I mean, besides the fact that you're . . . in this unique situation here at two o'clock in the morning. What's going on?"

After a long pause, during which the man looked anywhere but at me, he finally replied, "My girlfriend's up there."

"In the room?" I questioned.

He nodded. "She kicked me out."

While I was beyond intrigued, I knew better than to get in the middle of a lovers' quarrel, so I dispensed with the questions. It was all I could do to keep from laughing until we got security to finally walk the man back upstairs to his room and verify that everything was okay between the two lovers.

I had the next two days off, so I didn't see the couple, but I wondered about them often after that night.

Who says the youngsters have all the drama?

•   •   •

One thing that never fails to surprise me is how much our guests expect us concierges to know. I guess I should take it as a compliment that they think we are so astute and knowledgeable about generally everything, but there are times when our area of expertise falls a little short of the request. Of course, most Vegas visitors are distracted with everything there is to see and do, but nevertheless it can be quite funny.

Most guests can usually tell what the weather is going to be like by peering out of their window, or turning on the local news. Others either don't think to try those options or figure they'll call down to the concierge desk to ask how hot it is currently or how hot it's going to be later in the evening.

A colleague of mine decided to have a little fun on his last day before moving on to another job. We had a young, bubbly guest who'd been taking in the hottest Vegas shows and soaking up the sun's rays by the pool each day. She was always polite, and laughed a lot, so I believe he thought it was safe to assume he could joke around with her when she called to check the weather for the day.

"Please hold one minute, ma'am," my colleague said. "I'll get the report from the hotel meteorologist."

After a little pause and a bit of giggling, my co-worker got back on the phone and let the guest know how warm it was going to be, information he'd read straight off the front page of the newspaper the day.

The guest was grateful for the information, and a few minutes later, we saw her scamper through the lobby and onto the Strip. We couldn't help but laugh a little and wonder if we should tell her the truth of the matter when she returned.

It was all harmless, of course, but apparently we got distracted and didn't notice when she came back to the hotel that evening. A few days later when the same woman called down to get the day's weather forecast from the "hotel meteorologist," the concierge on duty was more than a little baffled! I had a few questions to answer the next day, and when I saw the lady at checkout, I finally broke down and told her how she'd been the butt of a little joke.

She waved her hand in front of her face and laughed. "That's okay," she said. "I should have known it was a silly question to be asking you anyway. I mean, I could just look it up myself. Next time, you just tell your guest who calls for a weather report that it's most likely partly cloudy with a chance of mirth." And she waved as she wheeled her luggage out of the door.

•   •   •

Back when I first became a Las Vegas concierge, I was assigned my first room set-up after a couple of weeks on the job.

The room in question was one of our deluxe honeymoon suites, and my job was to prepare it for a newlywed couple arriving later that day. However, there was a lack of communication from the front desk and unbeknownst to me — as I was busy arranging candles, rose petals, lotions, a massage table and more — the newly minted husband and wife checked into the hotel early and made their way upstairs.

My heart leapt into my throat when I heard the door burst open and then glimpsed the groom carrying his bride across the threshold. Luckily, because it was a suite, I happened to be in one of the adjoining rooms. Not knowing what to do, I hid behind a door. I was panic-stricken as I ran through the options of what to do next.

Perhaps I should clear my throat and walk out of the adjoining room? But what if the husband and wife were in the middle of a romantic moment? No one wanted to begin a honeymoon that way, and I certainly didn't want to witness the consummation of any marriage. The embarrassment I could face was almost too horrible to think about!

Maybe I could stay hidden and wait until the couple left the hotel room – but I had no idea how long that might take and eventually, my boss and co-workers would start to wonder where I'd gone. And look at where I was: the bedroom! The likelihood of the first scenario was even greater in there.

Also, what if I waited and then they found me, lurking in a closet or hiding behind the door? Surely it would be interpreted as a violation of the couple's privacy, and they would report me to my boss. I knew I had to get out of there soon, and I was about to simply start humming and walk out into the room as if I hadn't heard them come in, explain what I was doing, and welcome them to the hotel . . . earlier than they'd been expected.

Thankfully, the young couple decided to take in the beautiful balcony view, affording me the opportunity to sneak out of the room before being detected. When I told a colleague what had happened, the story was soon out among the staff, and I took a lot of ribbing from my colleagues over the whole thing. They teased me for days about now knowing what it felt like to be the "other woman."

But it was soon forgotten when this unlucky couple had an encounter with one of the maids in housekeeping.

I'd noticed the new husband lingering around my desk late one afternoon before he finally approached and asked directions to the Grand Canyon. I pulled out the map and talked him through the route, but he seemed unfocused on the information. Even after I'd answered his question, he lingered a bit longer and I noticed his eyes kept darting around.

"Is there something else I can help you with?" I asked politely.

He opened his mouth as if to say something and then closed it quickly. When the area was cleared of people, he leaned a little closer and finally whispered, "I've got to tell you something."

I immediately became worried. What if he'd seen me sneak out of the room while they were on the balcony? What if he was aware that I had been there when they came into the suite? My heart was pounding, but I assured him he could tell me.

"I'm very upset with your housekeeping department," he continued quietly. "We had a 'Do Not Disturb' sign on our door, but I'm afraid the maid came in anyway."

I immediately assured the young man that our housekeepers were very good about following proper procedure before entering.

"Oh, she knocked," he admitted, starting to blush, "but when we didn't answer, she unlocked the door and walked in."

"But if you heard her knock, why didn't you answer?" I asked, puzzled.

He leaned a little further toward me and said, "I was right in the middle of making love to my wife... and at exactly THAT moment, the maid showed up and . . . well, I couldn't very well just stop, you know what I mean?"

He looked pained as he provided his explanation, but I was experiencing some pain of my own trying to keep the laughter from spewing forth. Instead, I replied, "Sir, I'm so, so sorry that happened to you. Do you want me to call the manager so you can make an official complaint?"

"Absolutely not," the young man scoffed. I think he was horrified at the idea of having to relate the story to anyone else. "I am just very, very upset, and I wanted you to know about this. Perhaps you can clarify with housekeeping that when the 'Do Not Disturb' sign is out, they should comply."

I patiently thanked him for bringing the matter to my attention, but neglected to tell him that most of the staff already knew about this unfortunate episode of *coitus interruptus,* thanks to a very talkative and still-smiling maid.

• • •

One week, we had a large family staying at our hotel. Among their brood was an unusually talkative and out-going eight-year-old boy, Todd, with whom I enjoyed some very animated conversations. He educated me on the various carnivorous dinosaurs as well as the history of roller coasters and how the discovery of ice cream came about. The entire family was very outgoing, and we spoke every chance we got, even joking back and forth when an opportunity presented itself. On the final day of their stay, I was working in the concierge lounge over-seeing our continental breakfast when the family came in for their final meal at the hotel.

After they'd been seated for a few minutes, I heard them laughing loudly and looked over to see what the commotion was. They were nudging Todd in my direction, but uncharacteristically, he was acting very shy. Loudly enough for me to hear, Todd's dad said, "I will give you ten dollars if you do it."

Todd blushed and covered his face, then seizing the moment as only youth can, he peeked out at his dad and countered, "I'll do it for a hundred."

Sure enough, I watched the boy's father pull out a hundred-dollar bill. Todd immediately jumped to his feet, walked over to my desk, got down on one knee, and said softly, "Will you marry me?"

By that time, the entire breakfast crowd was paying attention and giggling at the sweet sight of a kid proposing to an adult female. They applauded his efforts and 'ooh'ed and 'ahhh'ed over the whole bit. Apparently, Todd had suffered at the hands of his family all week, taking the ribbing from his older brothers and sisters about his little crush on the helpful concierge.

The family was in hysterics as Todd rushed back to the table to grab his $100 bill. However, I figured he needed to do a little bit more to truly earn his pay.

I got up and crossed over to the family's table and tapped Todd on the shoulder. Kneeling down so that I was face-to-face with him, I said, "Todd, you left so quickly that I didn't have a chance to give you an answer."

Sheepishly, Todd looked at me and whispered, "You don't really have to if you don't want to."

I leaned forward and took his hand in mine. "Well, how about this: I'll marry you if you ask me again in twenty years."

Todd grinned and then looked up at his brothers proudly. They encouraged him with high-fives and laughter. The dad was so thrilled by my play-along spirit and the connection I'd obviously made with his son, that I too was rewarded with a nice, crisp one-hundred-dollar bill. I'm sure that was only the beginning of what his father shelled out years later when Todd really did get married.

• • •

A bunch of guys had come to Vegas for a bachelor party and wanted to prank the husband-to-be. The plan was to place a blow-up doll under the sheets in his room before he checked in. My task was to provide said blow-up doll, of course, so I ran to the adult store and bought one, a task I've done more times than the average person, I'm guessing.

When I got back to the hotel, I realized that I most likely wouldn't have time to blow up the entire thing by myself, and it wasn't as if I could sit behind my desk and work on blowing up this plastic nude woman while people came by to chat or called on the phone. The bachelor party would be arriving in less than an hour, so I needed to come up with a quick solution.

I began searching the closets, sure that I'd seen a tank when I'd cleaned the stock room previously. There it was, gleaming brightly in the corner and clearly marked, "helium." I attached it to the doll and in less than two minutes, the doll was fully inflated and ready for action.

I rushed up to the soon-to-be-husband's room and tucked it under the sheets, thinking the weight of the sheets and the comforter would hold the doll in place for the surprise, in spite of the helium inside it. Then I returned to my desk and went on about my business without giving it another thought.

A few hours later, I got a call from my general manager. He explained to me that a maid from our housekeeping staff had fainted upstairs and was being attended by paramedics.

"Can you call her daughter to come and pick her up?" he asked me. "We're going to send her home."

"What?" I asked. "That's horrible."

"Yes," he replied. "Apparently, the maid walked into a room and saw a dead body pressed against the ceiling."

His words were so bizarre that it took me a few moments to realize what he meant. I had to replay them in my head a few times and work to understand the sentence he'd uttered.

Then it hit me! The blow-up doll had somehow gotten free of the sheets and had floated up to the ceiling!

Yes, it's humorous now, but it's safe to say that my general manager didn't find it very funny at that moment, and I was beside myself that I had played a role in this sweet lady's receiving the shock of her life. My colleagues still occasionally ask about the day the blow-up doll... blew up in my face.

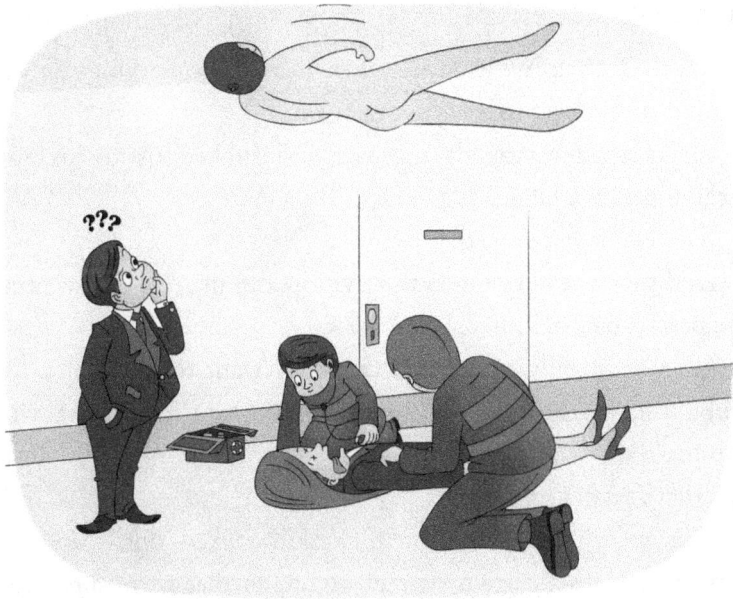

• • •

I was enlisted, quite innocently I might add, as a co-conspirator when a couple of guys named Matthew and David wanted to prank the rest of the guys in their group trip to Vegas. They approached the desk and said they had a special request.

"You see, last weekend, the two of us were left out of a boating trip by our buds. The reason was that the boats held only seven people each, but counting the ice chests, only six could fit. Our friends had to make a choice: us or the chests full of beer. We lost," the guest explained.

His friend picked up from there and told me the rest of the story.

"Of course, our friends apologized, but obviously we are still haunted by the memories," he laughed. "At least, we will be until we pay them back. We want to give them a little something that will remind them never to leave us out again."

He clapped his hands together and rubbed them, his eyes gleaming with a plan.

"Do tell," I encouraged.

And then they explained their vision and my role in executing the perfect payback.

"They've already mentioned that they want to frequent a few clubs, and we thought we'd suggest asking you for some advice," Dave told me.

"That's easy," I said.

"But we already have the nightclub picked out," Matthew explained. "It's a certain type of nightclub that we're sure you'd most likely never suggest unless you were asked specifically about it."

The plan was beginning to take shape in my mind, and I nodded in understanding.

As predicted, later on in the day, I was able to spend a moment with the whole group, and when the topic of the weekend and nightclubs came up, I inserted myself into the conversation quite naturally.

"The very best," I told them, "is this great little place right down the street. The drinks are reasonably priced, the atmosphere is very trendy. Everyone who goes there absolutely loves it. If you haven't been, it's a total MUST."

Matthew and Dave sat back nodding, saying it sounded like somewhere they should check out, and one of the other guys asked for the name of the club again. I felt confident we'd all played our parts quite well.

On Friday night, the two pranksters set the second part of their plan in motion. They told the rest of the group that they had another errand planned and that they'd meet them at the agreed-upon club.

Nothing was suspected as I watched a group of twelve gentlemen dressed to kill head out of the lobby and down the street to one of the most popular and lively gay bars in Vegas.

According to the story, about ten minutes after their arrival, a group of gay bikers pulled up in front of the bar and joined the crowd. The jig at that point was up, as the Rainbow Riders, fully dudded out in chaps and leather jackets, infused the bar and sidled up to the twelve newbies hoping to get acquainted.

But here's where I have to give the group credit. Instead of bolting at that point and getting angry at Matthew and Dave for the practical joke and awkwardness, they refused to leave. They chatted up the cyclists and the bartenders, and had a great time, and when Matthew called to ask where they were, they refused to go anywhere else on their last night unless the other two joined them for a drink there first.

No one in the group "came out" that night, which would really have been the icing on the prank cake, but who knows? Maybe next year.

•  •  •

When I first started working as a concierge, I wanted to make sure my guests could reach me at any time, especially if there was an emergency. For this reason, I gave one of my guests my cell phone number. I had been serving this guest for a few days and was helping with a particularly large project, so I wanted to make sure nothing went wrong.

He called one afternoon on my day off to check on a delivery that we had scheduled. Then later that evening, he called again, worried about a certain choice of flower we'd made. When I arrived at work the next morning, I had two messages from him already in regards to transportation, and I felt my cell phone buzz in my pocket with a text from him.

I was beginning to regret making myself this accessible to him, but the regret really came later that night.

I'd clocked out and gone home for the evening, having assured my guest that everything was going smoothly. At two o'clock in the morning, my cell phone jarred me from my sleep, and I sat upright in my bed, sure I was having a heart attack.

When I reached for my phone, I saw it was from the hotel, so I picked up quickly, hoping nothing was wrong.

"I wanted to know if you could get me into this particular club, and also maybe reserve a limo," my guest said, as if he had no idea what time it really was or that he'd most likely startled me from slumber.

It took me a moment to respond because I was still trying to calm my wildly beating heart. A number of responses crept through my head, but they would have been completely inappropriate for me to use. Finally, I told my guest that I didn't have access to my computer at the moment.

"I was actually sleeping, and I have to get up very early in the morning."

I'd had no idea how literally the guest would take it when I told him to "call if he needed something."

That's when I learned that concierges never give out their personal numbers. Doing so only means the end of personal time. Too bad I learned the hard way.

• • •

One of the many ploys used by casinos in Vegas is to keep the liquor coming. In fact, many casinos have free drinks available to the gamblers brought straight to the tables and slot machines because it'll keep them gambling. Of course, this results in various states of inebriation. When guests imbibe a bit too much, it's usually not a surprise, and anything that needs to be handled is done with tact by the concierge and security if need be. Forgotten room keys and other accidents are quite normal. However, one of my guests became very drunk one night at dinner, though I suspected he'd been in the casino and drinking long before then.

We have a piano player in our dining room, and as most guests were clearing out, he played a jaunty little upbeat tune. Suddenly, the intoxicated guest jumped up on the table and began performing a strip tease right then and there.

Of course, there was nothing I could do personally, but I knew I had to get this guest out of there! I called security, and they came as quickly as possible.

I could see the hesitation in the eyes of the three men when they arrived to the scene. In the time it had taken them to arrive, my guest had shed every single piece of his clothing and his hirsute body was jiggling all over the place with his movement. He was dancing very lewdly and unsteadily on the tabletop, knocking dishes over and causing all of those watching to shrink in fear . . . and perhaps a little disgust. He was extremely sweaty from the exertion, though he didn't seem embarrassed at all about sharing any of his assets.

I watched as the three security men looked back and forth at each other. You could almost hear their thoughts: *Are we going to have to tackle this hairy, drunk, naked guy? Do we actually have to put our hands on his body to get him out of here?*

I felt so sorry for them, especially the lead security officer who was an older, refined gentleman known for embarrassing quite easily. They conferred with each other, and after a few moments they came up with a plan and were able to get the job done, removing the drunken dancer from the dining room. I was just thankful it was nearly empty, but the few diners who had been present weren't offended. They were laughing and cheering the security guards, applauding their efforts, but mostly, I think they were just feeling lucky not to have been in their shoes.

# A Time for Miracles

## Longshots

It's a wonderful thing for a concierge to be able to make a dream come true. Whether it's ensuring that a guest has an amazing time, or delivering something the guest would never think possible – these are the moments when a concierge truly feels like he/she is serving a guest. It can be a privilege, an honor, and very emotional as well!

A female guest and her nine-year-old son had come to Las Vegas with her husband, who was participating in a convention. When she came to my desk to ask for a good kid-friendly place to go for lunch, it seemed to me like something was bothering her.

"Is there anything else I can do?" I asked her. There was a bit of a hesitation, and I sensed she wanted to say more. "Please, don't hesitate," I encouraged.

She looked at me a little crestfallen. "I have to confess, I absolutely hate this place. I can't stand it."

I was sure the shock showed on my face as this was the last thing I was expecting her to say. Still, I could tell she was unloading the truth—something I had the impression she hadn't felt okay to do with her husband for some reason. "I mean, the only reason we're here is because of my husband's convention, and he wanted to turn it into a family vacation. A family vacation in Vegas. I never would have agreed to this if it weren't for the fact that his job is paying part of the expenses. This place is a modern-age Sodom and Gomorrah."

I understood where she was coming from. Vegas can be a lot to digest, especially for people who are accustomed to a more conventional lifestyle.

I smiled at her and said, "Look, we can make things fun for you and your son. Believe it or not, Vegas can be a very family-friendly place. Let me take this as a personal challenge. Let me turn it around and make sure that you have a really good time."

"Good luck," she said, sarcastically.

"I'm serious," I insisted. "Just let me handle everything."

She held up her hands in surrender. "I doubt you can make it much worse," she told me, and I got right to work on showing her the softer side of Vegas.

First, I got tickets for the Hoover Dam, Red Rock Canyon, and Mount Charleston. I also got a few tickets for a beautiful circus show that I thought she and her son would both love. Then, for the last night, I got a licensed and bonded babysitter and provided the little boy with a bunch of great in-room movies so that the mother and father could go out and enjoy a nice dinner complete with champagne.

When the family was checking out, the woman approached me with a wide smile, her arms extended.

"Thank you so much!" she said as she hugged me. "I cannot believe how much I love this place now. You proved me completely wrong, and I think I had the best vacation of my life here."

The couple and their son have come back every year after that for a vacation, and I make sure to still challenge myself to show them how much they can fall in love with Las Vegas . . . as if it were the first time.

• • •

People like Vegas because they can lose their inhibitions— become the person they can't be at home—let the wild side through. Add to that a holiday like Halloween and there's no stopping some people. It's customary for concierges to help a fair share of guests find the right costume for Halloween or masquerade parties throughout the year. I remember one guy who was due at a costume party later in the evening, and he came to me for help.

"Well, do you want to dress as a celebrity?" I asked. "Or perhaps some iconic figure? Do you have favorite movies or characters?"

"I don't know. I don't really have time to watch movies like I used to," he confided. "Who do you think I look like?"

I snapped my fingers in inspiration. "John Travolta!" I said as I gazed at his thick, lush, black hair. "How about *Saturday Night Fever?*"

He smiled coyly. "I was known to have a few moves when I was younger," he confided.

I found the costume without a bit of trouble, and when he came sauntering into the expansive lobby, it was as if he had completely become Tony Manero. He literally slid over the polished hardwood floors to my desk and held his hand across the registration counter to me. When I came around, he swept me off my feet, dancing me all around the lobby doing moves from *Saturday Night Fever* in the process. Guests were pausing to watch and giggle, some applauding the impromptu performance.

*Oh my*, I thought. *I picked the wrong costume. This guy believes in the adage 'The clothes make the man!'* I love dancing, but . . . I wasn't counting on being his dance partner for the evening.

His attitude, I had to admit, was just great. He strutted around, completely convincing everyone that he was Tony Manero. His confidence was palpable as some of the guests began to snap pictures of the two of us. He had such a great time that he comes back every year now, and he greets me by saying, "I need my John Travolta costume, and you'd better be ready to dance!"

So every year, Mr. Travolta and I jig around the lobby while the guests laugh and take pictures. I can't help but form a picture in my mind of an 80-year old me dancing with a cane-bearing John Travolta – but it's memories like this that make the job so wonderful!

• • •

With all the weddings that take place in Las Vegas, odds are that a concierge is bound to find him/herself involved in a wedding dress fiasco. There are two that really stand out in my mind.

One morning, a bride-to-be walked up to my desk in her full wedding day attire. She looked stunningly beautiful: gorgeous dress, perfect shoes, fairytale hair – but she was crying hysterically and ruining her make-up.

"What's the matter?" I asked.

She couldn't say anything for all the sobbing, so she merely pointed dramatically to the anti-theft device still attached to the dress. Finally, I calmed her down enough to gather the details: she'd sent her dress out a few weeks earlier to be altered, and it had come back to the hotel with the device attached to the skirt. Somehow, she'd failed to notice this until the very last minute.

There were three things that made this situation much worse. The first was that the dress was a fitted dress and the fabric was very sleek, so there was no way to hide the device in the folds of the gown. The second was that it was one of those anti-theft capsules that would spill ink all over the garment if it was broken, so there was no strong-arming it. The third was that the bride's entire family (aunts, cousins, sisters) were standing in the lobby, nervously whispering back and forth to each other, and I was sure they were creating all sorts of stories to explain the hysterical bride in all her garb standing at my desk.

Since I had worked a short stint as a costume creator for a theater prior to my concierge career, I drew from that experience, immediately calling housekeeping for a sewing kit.

The whole time I was waiting for it, I was consoling the bride, assuring her that I had a background in sewing and designing and that I would do everything within my power to rectify the situation. All I needed was for her to trust me. Inside, however, I was thinking, *oh, man. What the hell am I going to do?*

When the kit arrived, I saw that I had a few spools of thread, some scissors, and a needle to work with – no miracle anti-theft-capsule-removing tool, unfortunately, but in a pinch it would all have to do. I dropped to my knees and got to work, wasting no time and cooing reassuringly to the bride who was beginning to reign in the sobs. I may have smiled up at her, but it was just me trying to look calm in the midst of the storm of anxiety I was feeling. The whole time I was thinking, *What if I ruin this gown? How much is it going to cost me? And don't even forget that it would ruin this woman's entire wedding day if I ruin this dress.*

I took a deep breath to steady my nerves and began cutting the fabric near the anti-theft device. I could hear gasps behind me, and one of the aunties whispered, "Oh dear lord, she's cutting the dress. I hope she knows what she's doing."

Inside, I answered the auntie: *Me, too.* I could almost feel the panic of the watching family travel through the bride and into me, but I tried with all my might to block it all out and channel every designer I had ever studied.

Although I'm fairly confident about my seamstress skills, I really started to second-guess myself, but I had passed the point of no return, so I kept going until I had cut the device out of the dress. Inspired, I stole some fabric from the hemline so I could patch up the spot where I'd operated. My boss then walked into the room and absorbed the situation. Kneeling down beside me for a moment, he whispered, "Are you sure you know what you're doing?"

I felt like asking him to wipe the sweat from my upper lip and hand me the needle, just like a good nurse would do for the operating surgeon, but instead, I just nodded. In a few more minutes, I had the hole patched up perfectly. Without seriously close inspection, you could never tell it had been cut in the first place. The bride was thrilled, and after the wedding, they ordered me flowers and showered me with gratitude. A few weeks later, I was voted Hotel Employee of the Month. I will always believe it was directly related to my mad skills with a needle and thread . . . and saving the bride's wedding day.

•    •    •

Another wedding dress fiasco ended with quite the pay-off for the bride. Many Las Vegas brides-to-be arrive ahead of their wedding dresses, planning to either shop for one in Las Vegas or take receipt of the gown after they have arrived. One couple who checked in were scheduled to get married a few days after their arrival, on a Sunday. The bride's wedding dress arrived the day before, on a Saturday. However, the couple was out all day and didn't return to their room until late Saturday night.

When the bride opened the package to inspect it, she found, much to her shock and almost debilitating dismay, a completely different dress: wrong color, wrong style, wrong size. The company had somehow sent her another woman's bridal gown, and there was no telling where her wedding dress was. Of course, it was now the middle of the night, and there was no way to order another gown. She came to me absolutely distraught.

"We're supposed to get married in the morning," she cried, "and now I have no wedding dress!"

I called every single wedding boutique I could find in the phone book, but none of them were open. I slammed the phone receiver down in frustration just as a colleague walked by.

"Wow. I've never seen you this frustrated. What gives?"

I told him about the dilemma and how horrible I felt for the bride.

"No problem," he said as he pulled out his cell phone.

119

My eyes bulged. "No problem?" I questioned. "How can you say, 'No problem'?"

He wrote down a name and number on a piece of paper and slid it over to me. "Because I have a very good friend who owns a great boutique. Give him a call; tell him I sent you; tell him the story. I know he'll help you out."

Feeling slightly hopeful but cautious, I gave the friend a call, and sure enough, he came out, opened up his shop, and we took the guest to meet him. All of this was happening well past midnight! To make matters even better, she found a dress she loved even more than the original, and since the original store had shipped her the wrong wedding dress, she received a full refund with them, enough to cover the cost of the new dress *and* a large chunk of her Hawaiian honeymoon! Who says the house always wins?

•   •   •

We concierges hate having to say "no" to a client (unless it means keeping one or both of us out of jail, of course). There are times, however, when it seems like the cards are stacked against us. That's when networking can often help, and if I've learned anything, it's that it pays to help each other out in the service industry. After all, you never know when you'll need to call in a favor.

One such time was when a young Hungarian couple came to Las Vegas, and told me how much they wanted to see Celine Dion. It just so happened that it was one of the last weekends of her Caesar's Palace contract, and without prior reservations, I had to tell them that it was practically mission impossible.

Still, I was determined to exhaust all my resources before giving up. With only a day or so to work with, I pled my case all the way up to the top of the Caesar's Palace food chain, explaining how much a pair of tickets would mean to my European guests. Understandably, there was nothing they could do.

Late the next afternoon, my Blackberry buzzed with an email notification that Caesar's had received a last-minute cancellation for Dion's Saturday show. The Hungarian couple could not believe their good fortune and neither could I. We were all thrilled that they were able to make the show, and I know that show definitely made their trip much more memorable.

There was also the time a high-roller approached the concierge desk at 7:15pm and asked for ringside seats to the heavyweight boxing event that was scheduled to start at 8pm!

Usually, these fights are completely sold out months in advance, and it was no different for this one. However, I had resources that the Average Joe didn't have. I dialed the cell phone number of the owner of a major ticket brokering firm on the Strip. It turned out that he was at the location where the fight would take place, and he had a few tickets on him.

I quickly explained the situation.

"Send him on!" my ticket broker friend said happily. "I'll be waiting for him."

The seats weren't quite ringside, but the guest was still happy . . . at least, happy enough to pay $6,000 per ticket! He had a great time at the event, and thanked me numerous times for getting the tickets. It was just great to get another knock-out under my belt!

But the most personal account of networking within the service industry came when a former colleague of mine called me from her home in the Philippines. Her brother had been working on a cruise ship, and while the ship was docked at an Italian port, he'd been arrested. The family was distressed and didn't know what to do. On top of that, they were having a difficult time communicating because of language barriers, so they were worrying themselves to death trying to get details and figure out what to do.

"Don't you have a cousin who is a police officer in Italy?" she asked me.

Immediately, I told her I'd give my cousin a call, and we'd see what we could find out. When I got in touch with my cousin, I explained the problem. He was able to guide my ex-colleague through the arcane Italian process of getting her brother released.

It had all turned out to be a big misunderstanding; the Italian authorities thought the man was someone else, and they apologized when they released him. As you can imagine, the family was so relieved, and my ex-colleague thanked me profusely for helping. It was a situation where I was able to help a fellow concierge, as well as the poor family who couldn't get any information. You just never know how much you're going to be able to help a person . . . even those who aren't guests.

•  •  •

One day I got a call from a man called Peter, who said to me, "I have to tell you a little story so you'll understand my request. When I was ten years old..."

My first reaction was, *Oh, dear. This is going to be a loooooong story.*

He continued, "That summer, my best friend's mom made him this snowman doll. Now, boys that age aren't supposed to like those kinds of things, but I really thought the doll was super-cool. He took it to his father's with him that summer, to remind him of home. When I went to summer camp the next summer, his mom sent the doll so that I'd have something to remind me of my friend.

"Over the years, it became a bit of a joke between us. We'd send it to each other every single summer, and even if we didn't talk much that year, it became a way for us to keep in touch. Well, for some reason, my friend hasn't sent me the snowman doll in about three years, but I decided to take matters in my own hands. I called up his mom, and she has gone into his house and 'stolen' the doll. Now I have it in my possession. Here's where you come in," he said. "My friend is staying in your hotel, and I'd like to overnight the doll to you and have you deliver it to him as a surprise."

I perked up quickly. "I love this sort of thing," I told the man on the phone. "The story is charming, and I'd be glad to help you with the surprise."

We made the arrangements for me to deliver the doll to his friend on the man's birthday, which was in a few days. I called Peter when the doll arrived.

"Where's John right now?" he asked me.

I said, "He's out by the pool."

"Can you take the doll out to the pool and sing 'Happy Birthday' to him?" he asked.

I chuckled a little and then shrugged. It wasn't the worst thing I'd ever been asked to do.

So, I took the snowman doll out by the pool and put on a little puppet act, singing "Happy Birthday" to John. No doubt his friends wondered what in the world was going on, but when John saw the snowman doll, he was over the moon.

"I can't believe this," he said. "My friend hasn't sent me that doll in three years. I kind of thought we were drifting. That's incredible."

"Well," I began, "the way I understand it, this doll has been in your possession for the last three years, and while you have been vacationing here in Las Vegas, Peter conspired with your mother to break into your house, steal the doll, and get the 'snowball' rolling again."

John couldn't believe it. Neither could Peter when I explained that John had thought he'd had the doll all this time.

I ended up telling both of them that they should call the other to catch up, and they each promised they would. I was just happy to have helped the friends reconnect after their misunderstanding.

•  •  •

I was enlisted to help a guy who wanted to propose to his girlfriend. The heart does not acknowledge price tags, but the guy had just a hundred bucks to make it happen. Of course, like any other guy, he wanted it to be special for his special lady. I rolled the number around in my head a bit, and then nervously asked the man if he already had the ring. Thank goodness, it was a yes! After a bit of thinking, I set to work on a plan inspired by the well-known wedding tradition of using "something old, something new, something borrowed, something blue".

We actually had a car rental at our hotel, so I went to the agent and told the story, asking whether she could provide a discount on a car.

"I think I can help you there," she said as she worked out some numbers. "How about thirty-five dollars?"

I was flabbergasted. "Any chance I can get that in a blue?" I grinned, hoping that I wasn't pushing my luck.

"Done!" she told me, giddy with excitement that she was helping to make a marriage proposal possible.

With that out of the way, I called another hotel in Las Vegas and spoke to the chef, again telling the story and asking if a set menu could be created for sixty dollars or less, including the tip. So a special menu was created for the couple; a dish, dessert, and coffee for two at the special price. Everything was falling into place!

I spent a fair amount of time coaching our guy on what he should say and do so that the theme was preserved, and on the night of the proposal, they took the car to the restaurant, had a delicious meal, and then they took a moonlit walk around the lake.

Together, the guest and I had written out the story of how they had met as if it were a fairy tale, complete with "once upon a time" and the allusion to "happily ever after". He told the story as they took their romantic walk, and when he returned to the car, he gestured at it.

"Of course you know this car is borrowed," he told the girl. "Did you notice it was blue?"

She looked at him in the moonlight. "What's that old saying?" she said, already feeling the familiarity of the words, as we'd hoped and planned.

He went down on one knee, "The ring is new, but I want to grow old with you," he said as he placed it on her finger.

"So here we have something old—if you'll have me—something new; something borrowed, and something blue. It's nothing spectacular, nothing over the top, but it's straight from my heart, and I'm giving you all that I've got. Will you marry me?"

With tears in her eyes and her heart in her throat, the girl agreed to marry him, and they kissed under the moon, the perfect moment in his creative proposal.

Unfortunately, during all my planning, I had completely forgotten that they would need to fill up the gas tank in the rental car before returning it, and the girl ended up paying for the gas. Perhaps it was the perfect first lesson about the give and take of love!

• • •

Speaking of the give and take of love, I got a panicked call one day from a man right across the country.

"My wife is on her way there. I arranged everything and packed everything for her. But I completely forgot something of terrible importance. It's a CD with thunder effects for a private concert performance my wife is scheduled to be part of!"

I calmed the caller down and got his phone number, then told him I'd see what I could do. It was Sunday morning, so there were no audio or video shops open at that point. However, I had theater experience and still had a few contacts from those days, so I called up one of my friends who was working on a local stage show version of Mamma Mia.

"I have a huge emergency," I told him, and then I explained the situation.

Before long I had a CD with thirty-five different thunder sound effects, and the guest hadn't even checked into the hotel yet! I left a little note on the CD and placed it in the guest's room. It said, "By now you may or may not have figured out that you've forgotten your sound effects CD. Here is one with plenty of thunder effects. I hope it's useful."

A few moments after checking in, the woman came down to my desk beaming.

"You're amazing! I didn't even have a chance to realize I needed to panic before you'd already provided the solution," she said.

"I hope the sound effects are to your liking," I told her. She waved her hand. "These are better than the ones I would have brought myself," she told me. "I love it!"

Later that night, she stopped in to tell me that the concert symphony had gone off without a hitch. The next day, a bouquet of yellow roses adorned my desk with a note that said, "Thank you. You're a life-saver!"

Today, whenever people ask me what I can do for guests, I sometimes trot out the line, "I'll get you thunder and lightning, if necessary. It's just a little something I've done before!"

• • •

It was New Year's Eve, and a particular woman known by the staff for her style and grace was staying in our hotel. She had gone out and purchased a very expensive designer dress for the big party and was excited about getting all dolled up and looking her best at the stroke of midnight. At about ten that night, the woman called my desk in a panic. She'd purchased a specific bra to wear under her designer dress, but she couldn't find it anywhere. She had only a few minutes before she had to leave for her party.

"Are there any stores still open?" she asked breathlessly.

"At this hour on December thirty-first? No," I replied, "none of them are going to have that kind of specialized merchandise."

I felt horrible for this woman because a bra was going to ruin her whole night.

"I can't wear a regular bra," she told me. "It's one of those criss-cross ones with removable straps. I certainly can't go braless. I just can't bring myself to do it," she said, disappointed.

"Oh, I know exactly what you're talking about," I said. "I wear the same kind."

"Wait," she said. "Are you wearing it now?"

Chuckling, I replied, "As a matter of fact, I am."

She immediately jumped on the opportunity, asking what cup size I wore and if she could borrow the bra. Of course, in a strange twist of fate, mine was the exact same size as hers. In a matter of minutes, the distressed guest was dressed, complete with my bra, and I went the rest of my shift with my suit jacket buttoned tightly over my bra-less bosom. I may not have given her the shirt off my back, but in my book, it was the next best thing. All in the name of service!

# Unusual Requests

## Propositions

Most Las Vegas concierges won't blink an eye at some of the requests that ordinary people might find a little strange. It's all part of the job, whether it's going out to find a strange food in the middle of the night or finding tickets to a specific show. However, as you'll quickly see, some of the requests made to concierges stick in their minds for a long, long time.

It's not uncommon for a guest to reach out to the concierge before he/she arrives at the hotel. Perhaps there are some needs that must be met prior to their arrival, or perhaps the guest has a very tight schedule and wants to insure everything will go seamlessly. I recall one such email from a man who would be arriving at our hotel, only his stay was going to be less than twenty-four hours.

His email started off normally, inquiring about whether or not transportation was available to and from the airport. I thought nothing about it as his inquiry was quite normal.

Then it all changed. After a few ordinary inquiries, his tone shifted, and the guest began describing issues that might affect his stay. He informed me that he had a "very weak immune system," and that meant he was at risk for "collateral damage". My anxiety levels increased as I wondered how we were going to prevent "collateral damage" to this guest. The email went on to list his allergies, which included but were not limited to cigarette smoke, molds, fungus, yeast, wheat, oats, barley and rye.

"I can't even be around any smokers," he informed me, "because they shed whatever it is I'm allergic to."

He went on to explain that he was "anaphylactic" towards any type of shellfish as well as a variety of nuts, not to mention that certain fragrances and colognes would bring on sudden asthma. I began wondering how much responsibility he was placing on me as a concierge. Surely he wasn't anticipating my tying him up and force-feeding him shrimp and lobster in peanut sauce while coating him in cologne? But, hey, he didn't know me.

*In addition* to all those allergies, he also couldn't have any type of dairy product, including anything that contained whey or caffeine. He was also highly allergic to chocolate—that one broke my heart for the poor fellow— and artificial sweeteners. In his own words, he was also, "essentially allergic" to alcohol as well, and he was unable to tolerate any spices other than salt and pepper.

He was allergic to synthetics and required only cotton sheets. (Finally, something I could control!) And he felt it imperative for me to know that he could eat only broiled meats, fresh fruits, steamed vegetables and eggs, and drink only water. He ended the email with a plea from his wife, who would appreciate it if he arrived home safely rather than in a pine box.

The end.

I felt exhausted and quite anxious considering he had placed all of this responsibility on my shoulders.

There was an afterthought, a postscript after his closing, in which he asked if we had adequate facilities and whether he should come prepared for the worst case scenario. For a second I wondered if he'd gotten himself confused; this was Las Vegas, not Laos.

There it was: the grin I'd been hoping for at the end of the email. This was something I could handle. I replied to his email with assurance that our facilities were state-of-the-art and very modern, and that I would happily have cotton sheets on the bed in his non-smoking room. I felt confident I could help him find a restaurant that could accommodate his dietary needs, and I told him to tell his wife we'd do our best to get him back safely and pine-box free.

*As for the shellfish, caffeine, alcohol, and various sundry food allergies, I thought, I'll let you worry about yourself there.*

When the guest checked in, I found myself gaping at him in wonder. The visual image I had conjured of him was so incredibly far from the truth. I admit it; I had relied on stereotypes. I thought with all the allergies and the status of "high maintenance" as well as the fearful wife, the man who would check in would arrive in a rumpled brown suit, a few years out of fashion and a size too large for his stooped frame. He'd be shorter than average with a hooked nose and bird-chest, and his greying, once-dark hair would be plastered to his balding head in a comb-over style that would convey his tenacious grip on preserving whatever youth he could.

In reality, however, he stood over six feet tall, with a barrel chest, the broad shoulders of a Greek god and the chiseled features to match. His dark mane fell almost to his shoulders, and I could feel myself smoldering under the gaze of his icy blue eyes.

*How's that for irony?* I asked myself. And though I—and a few other staffers who were lucky enough to catch a glimpse of this man's magnificence—had a fleeting visual of our own plans and desires for him, I am happy to report that we were able to provide him with everything he needed... and he went home by airplane, pine box not included!

• • •

People assume that a concierge in Vegas gets outrageous, kinky requests, but believe it or not, the majority of the requests that are outrageous are not that kinky. Once, I had the chance to meet a very famous boxer while he was in Las Vegas. He was a super-nice guy, and we were excited to have him staying with us. Off duty, I ran into him at a popular Vegas night club. He invited me over, and I found myself sitting at his table, hobnobbing with him and some of his friends. Everyone who is anyone in Vegas stopped by the table that night just to say hello and wish him well. I felt like I was "somebody"!

It seemed friend after friend bought him a drink, and finally, after several rounds, he leaned over to me and my friend who'd accompanied me and said, "Can you get me out of here?"

Always a concierge, my desire to serve kicked in even though it was my night off.

"Give me your room key," I instructed him as I tried to concoct a plan, but he shook his head.

"I don't want to go to my room. I want to get a grilled cheese sandwich."

I stood still in a moment of shock; this was the last request I'd expected from him. He named a popular fast-food chain, got his money out, and asked if I had a car.

A quick vision of my old, two-door Honda flashed through my head, and I tried to envision getting this mammoth guy into the backseat. Not only had my car seen better days, but it had also not seen the likes of this guest, and I wasn't too sure he'd want to eat anything after riding in my car with me.

Reluctantly, my friend and I led him to the car and put him in the backseat. I couldn't believe that I had a world-famous boxer— who incidentally had just dropped several thousand dollars in a nightclub— ducking his head and crawling into the backseat of my old car.

I got him to the fast-food joint and ordered his grilled cheese for him—several, in fact. Then the moment of hilarity struck me, and I couldn't stop laughing as he inhaled the bag of grilled cheese sandwiches he'd ordered.

"You know," I said, "I can't believe we're doing this. We could have gone back to your room and had room service deliver you a dozen grilled cheese sandwiches. But instead, here you are, squeezed into my ratty little Honda so that you can get a sandwich from a drive-thru."

"What can I say?" he answered, his mouth stuffed with cheese and bread and grease. "They make the best here!"

They say you can't buy happiness; we've all heard that before. But in that moment, I knew it wasn't true, for I had one blissful millionaire sitting in the backseat of my Honda, happier than a clam. For him, a few dollars had bought happiness in the form of toast and melted cheese! And I was just happy I got to help make it all happen.

•   •   •

There's a certain freedom that exists in Las Vegas, and when people come, they want to take advantage of it before returning to their "normal" lives. One such guest was willing to make the most of her visit, and she approached me as soon as she had settled herself into the hotel.

"I need some information," she said.

"Well, you've come to the right place," I smiled. "What can I help you with?"

"It's a bit crazy," she prefaced, "but I'd like the contact information for Cher's plastic surgeon."

Immediately, I had a vision of the woman standing before me waltzing back into the hotel with high cheekbones and a long sheet of dark hair and somehow another four inches of height. I blinked the image away, but the guest didn't bat an eye.

"Do you think you can find that out for me?" she asked hopefully.

"I'll do my very best. It may take me some time, but when I have some information, I'll let you know." I had her write down her name and room number so that I could contact her, and she gave me a warning as she scribbled out the information.

"Now, it's imperative we get the info as soon as possible. I can't stay in Vegas forever, you know."

I began searching the Internet as she walked away, skimming through our personal resources, calling the plastic surgeons I knew. I even pulled some strings in the entertainment industry to get names of plastic surgeons to the stars.

No one appeared to know who Cher's plastic surgeon was, or if they did, they were keeping it secret. Apparently, this celebrity either doesn't want to share her plastic surgeon, or when she has surgery done, it's far from The Strip!

Finally, I called the guest's room. "I'm sorry," I reported. "I can't find the contact information, not even a name!" I confessed. "I hate to say it, but I've got zilch, babe."

The guest left for home looking almost exactly the same as when she had arrived – maybe a little more tan and a lot more relaxed, which I thought was just as good as some high-dollar plastic surgeon.

• • •

Believe it or not, guests' pets are some of our harshest critics, and we want everything to be as perfect for them as it is for their owners. Once, there was a particular guest at the hotel who had a very spoiled little dog. "Fond" does not even begin to explain the feelings this woman had for her dog, and vice versa, I'm sure. Any time we saw the guest, her little dog was trotting alongside her all around the hotel, in and out of the door, riding the elevator. But what was different about this dog was that she was dressed to the nines, outfitted in diminutive skirts, little bitty sweaters, and always her signature tiny, custom-made, pink leather booties. (Well, those Vegas sidewalks get very hot!) In fact, it was on a very hot Las Vegas day that the guest decided to cool off with a swim. Naturally, she expected to have the dog at her side, as usual. She called down to the concierge desk.

"I am in need of an inflatable raft, that will hold both myself and my dog, to be delivered to the pool," she instructed. This was back in the 80s before people even thought twice about having a dog in the pool. After all, this was before we'd become allergic to everything or overly-cautious about sanitation.

My wheels began turning as I envisioned the proper dimensions of a raft that would hold both owner and dog without being too obtrusive to the other guests who may want to enjoy the pool. My colleague found a suitable raft, but unfortunately, none of us—dog-owner included— had completely thought through this endeavor. As soon as the dog got near the pool, it jumped in, ruining those beautiful little pink boots.

I think the dog's owner was more distraught at the ruination of the booties than the dog was. Immediately, a new quest was assigned, and I was tracking down a local cobbler.

"I have a guest who needs a pair of leather booties made for her dog," I explained.

Silence... I could almost hear the confusion running through his head.

"Hello?" I asked, thinking that maybe he had hung up on me.

"Is this for real?" he asked.

"It is," I assured him. "I can have one of the originals sent over as a pattern, but they got ruined when the dog jumped in the pool."

More silence.

"Are you there?" I asked.

"Leather booties for a dog?" came the question.

"Yes. *Pink* leather booties," I clarified. "The guest is very adamant that they be pink. And she would like them as soon as possible."

"This is going to be one expensive order," he told me. "Custom-made pink leather booties in a quick turnaround time? That's racking up quite the bill," he said.

"What can I say?" I replied. "It's all in the name of fashion!"

• • •

Being a concierge means being a part of a tight-knit group of professionals that wraps all around the world. It's like a membership into an exclusive club, and one of the perks of that membership is being able to call on each other for help at any given moment anywhere in the world.

My phone rang one day, and I heard a friend's voice on the other end saying, "I know you'll do anything for *your* guests, but what about the guests of your concierge friends?"

I laughed, and answered that I'd be a horrible friend if I didn't at least do for my fellow concierges (and consequently their guests) what I would for perfect strangers.

"Great!" he smiled. "Just the answer I wanted to hear."

"Uh-oh," I shot back. "What have I just gotten myself into?"

My friend explained that he had a guest, Kevin, an attorney, who had big plans for his girlfriend's birthday.

"The hitch is, Elena is an eight-hour drive from you, and Kevin is here in New York, all the way across the country."

I saw my involvement taking shape.

"He's purchased two puppies that are waiting to be collected not far from your hotel."

"Let me guess," I interrupted, "he wants me to make sure Elena gets the puppy package?"

"Exactly," my friend conceded. "He actually contacted a few courier services out there, but none of them would agree to deliver live animals. So, I told Kevin that I had a friend in Vegas who was a great concierge with many resources available, and I thought you might be able to pull some strings to make this happen."

I had to admit: I was flattered, but I was also up against the clock. I didn't get off work for another hour, and the hotel where Elena was staying was over eight hours away. Not to mention that I still had to find and pick up the puppies in the first place.

"He's never missed a birthday," my friend explained, "and he already feels horrible that they're separated by practically an entire continent. Is there anything you can do?"

I understood, and I felt for Elena, too. Everyone wants to be remembered on their birthday. So, I told my friend to get Kevin to write a heart-felt love letter and fax it over to me with the information on where to pick up the puppies, as well as details of Elena's hotel. As soon as I got the requested information, I contacted the concierge there and began to make arrangements with her.

There was an adorable boutique store across the street, and I enlisted them to fashion these beautiful bows for the puppies. Finally, I was able to hire a limo driver to deliver the puppies to Elena's hotel. The limo driver kept me updated during his eight-hour drive, and I filled him in on the details I'd worked out with the other concierge. When the puppies finally arrived, the concierge at Elena's hotel attached the beautiful bows to the puppies and delivered them to Elena's room with the love note Kevin had faxed me.

The concierge at Elena's hotel called me and my friend, and the three of us reveled in the story of how we were able to help one hotel guest on one side of the continent thrill and surprise another hotel guest on the opposite side of the continent.

"She was crying!" the other concierge reported. "Tears of joy, of course. But because she hadn't heard from Kevin all day and the package was delivered so late — at 11 p.m. — she had convinced herself that he'd forgotten all about her birthday."

"I think it contributed to the intensity that it arrived so late in the evening," I added. "But I'm so glad we were able to pull it all off!"

"Who needs Superman when you've got the Powers of the Concierge?" my friend asked, and we all laughed, happy that we were able to help make a most memorable birthday even from across the continental United States.

• • •

If you haven't noticed already, a concierge must be ready for anything. We wear many hats and keep a long list of contacts and suitable resources for a variety of scenarios and occasions. Sometimes we have to pull off some last-minute magic, and for some reason, this usually translates: flower power!

It's not uncommon for wedding receptions to happen in our hotel, and there has been more than one occasion when the pre-ordered arrangements haven't made it to the hotel on time. This means that we often have to make do with what we can find at the local grocery store. Though it doesn't rival anything that a professional florist can create, I have to say that we don't do too badly in a pinch. We pick the boldest, freshest flowers, buy the most modern vases we can find, and then cut and arrange the flowers to fit. No one's ever been anything but thrilled.

But here's a little secret that even the particular bride in this situation never knew. More than once, when there is nothing suitable at the local grocery, we have had to make do with some very creative solutions. For example, one week we had a wedding party staying at the hotel and when the boutonnieres they'd ordered arrived—extremely late, no less—the flowers for the gentlemen turned out to be all wrong.

"The bride specifically said 'no pink', and here are the boutonnieres—all shades of pink," the wedding planner told us. "She will absolutely freak when she sees these. She hates pink more than any color and has been adamant about avoiding it."

We called every florist we knew, but the wedding was less than an hour away.

"I don't know what other option we have," I said to the planner, who was just beginning to pull her hair out. "Can you speak with the bride and see if there's any possible way she can overlook it, just for a bit?"

But she shook her head vigorously from side to side. "Nope. No way. We must figure something out. I think she'd rather go without the boutonnieres than have the pink roses," she countered.

And I shrugged, reconciling myself to being the one to explain that there were no boutonnieres for the groomsmen.

"Can't we just make them ourselves?" a staffer asked me.

I looked into her eyes, and a brilliant plan dawned. While I instructed a few staffers to find pins and floral tape, I tracked down the groundskeeper to borrow his pruning shears. I went to the many rose bushes that flanked each side of the grand entryway inside the lobby atrium and carefully cut eight of the most perfect red roses I could find. With the baby's breath from the florist's boutonnieres and the red roses from the hotel's own bushes, we made eight boutonnieres in less than an hour, and they looked completely professional!

More importantly, the bride was never the wiser, and her perfect day went off without a hitch.

•　　•　　•

Sometimes it isn't even the guests at our own hotels who make a lasting impression. A guest who was actually staying at another hotel in another state called and put in a request that I will never forget.

"There's a lady who will check in tomorrow," he informed me, "and I'd like to surprise her." He —let's call him Mr. Smith — continued outlining his detailed plan for the next few minutes without any pause for me to interject. His request included having a certain poem written in calligraphy on the mirror. The other aspects of his surprise for this lady — let's call her Ms. Jones — included a single rose which should be placed by the mirror, and the song "La Comparsita" playing upon her entry to the room.

"First, let me talk with housekeeping about a few red flags and how we might avoid them," I told him. I promised to get back to him within a few hours' time, and set to work on making his vision become a reality.

After speaking with housekeeping and some other staffers, I called him back.

"So, the poem on the mirror poses a bit of a problem," I explained, and proceeded to tell him the housekeeping staff's concerns. "My plan, however, is to go out and get an inexpensive mirror that could be placed in the room with the poem written in calligraphy. "Afterwards, housekeeping said they would clean it up if necessary, or if Ms. Jones would like, she can take the mirror with her with the poem still intact."

"Perfect! That's even better!" Mr. Smith confirmed. He apparently liked the idea that Ms. Jones could keep it as a memento should she choose to.

"I've been brainstorming a few other ideas," he informed me. "I'd like to have a drawing or, better yet, a painting of a couple dancing placed next to the mirror with the poem. If possible, both the man and the woman in the painting should have dark hair, and I'd like the woman to be wearing a blue dress."

I was taking notes as fast as I could, but already my mind was scrolling through my list of resources. Who could I find on such short notice to help me out with this special surprise?

With less than twenty-four hours to pull this off, I went out and bought the CD with the song, then rented a CD player from the audio/video department, and set up the song to play on repeat so that it would be playing upon Ms. Jones's arrival.

With the mirror and the rose also in the works, I needed to focus on the last-minute addition: the illustration to accompany the poem.

I was fortunate because at the time, the hotel had just had a beautiful mural painted by a great local artist. I wasn't sure about her timeline and how close she was to completing the project, but I went to track her down. My heels were click-clacking through the lobby and lower hallways towards the bank of elevators where the work was being done.

Unfortunately, I found the mural complete, and when I asked around, I learned she'd been gone for a week already.

Bummer.

Slowly, I began walking back to my office, the wheels in my head turning as I wondered how in the world I could pull this all together. I'd been concentrating so hard on my own plans that I almost walked right into someone, and when I finally focused enough on what I was doing, I saw who it was.

It was the artist, coming to pick up her final paycheck, and I had literally almost run her over, lost in my thoughts about who I'd contact now that she was gone.

"Am I glad to see you!" I said.

"And am I glad you finally did see me," she responded with a smile.

I apologized and told her all about my dilemma. "And so, I was just coming to find you to see if you could help me out with this."

She nodded. "I can do a small painting," she said, "but it will need to dry for an entire day".

"Great!" I clapped my hands and turned her body by the shoulders so that she could walk beside me. "Let's get started on it right now!"

We got her the supplies she requested, and she completed the painting right then and there!

With everything placed perfectly and the song playing in the background, I filled in my colleague since I'd be off the next day, which was when Ms. Jones would be arriving.

The next morning, before I was fully coherent, I received a call from the concierge on duty.

"Ms. Jones just checked in," the concierge informed me.

"Great," I yawned.

"She's with a man," he whispered, "and the man's name is not Mr. Smith; nor does he have dark hair."

I flashed to the painting of the couple dancing, and then I began to panic. Were we in cahoots with a paramour? My chest felt tight as I began running through all the possible scenarios and issues. We couldn't tell Mr. Smith that Ms. Jones had arrived because Mr. Smith might be the husband. Or, perhaps Ms. Jones was here with her husband, and Mr. Smith was a lover. Could Mr. Smith even be a past lover who was still smitten with and still stalking Ms. Jones? It was a very awkward situation.

"Okay, here's what we're going to do," I said to the concierge. "Do we have another room available that's comparable to the one she reserved?"

I heard the clicking of the keyboard as he checked and confirmed that we did.

"Check her into that room," I instructed. "Then, call her once she's in and tell her there was something private prearranged for her and her eyes only."

Later the concierge called her. "Ms. Jones, we have a surprise for you, but it's very private—only for you," he told her. "If you could get away for a moment, the concierge will escort you to the surprise."

When the concierge opened the door to the other room for Ms. Jones, she began to cry.

"She was very moved," he told me, "and she said that the surprise was very beautiful. She wanted to move to what we now called 'the surprise room.'" (Who could blame her? Mr. Smith had already paid for an upgraded suite.)

Later, Mr. Smith called me on my personal phone (I had given him the number since I would be off for the day) to see how the surprise went. I was able to tell him that Ms. Jones had been extremely surprised and touched—though I was careful not to mention the other man or the changing of the rooms.

I'm still not quite sure what the situation was, but since then, I've followed my own policy: I don't put anything into any guest's room if it's not been requested by them specifically! It's just better on my heart that way. After all, love is a many "splintered" thing, and sometimes those splinters can hurt the innocent concierge in the process.

• • •

Believe it or not, we get a lot of requests for white doves. After all, they are a highly recognized symbol of love, commitment and purity, and there's just something about the magic in the city of Las Vegas that gets couples feeling quite "lovey dovey" if you will.

One time, I had a guest who had come to Las Vegas with the intention of proposing to his girlfriend. He planned to take her to the top of the Paris Hotel and Casino's Eiffel Tower for the most romantic view of the city as the setting.

"What I'd really love to do," he told me, "is to have someone release seven white doves when I get down on my knee and ask the big question. And I want the moment captured on film, too."

As a hopeless romantic, I practically swooned with the images that were swirling around in my head, but as a concierge, I knew there would be some strings we'd have to pull if we wanted this proposal to go the way he was envisioning it.

"Let me get to work," I told him, and I called the Paris concierge to begin making arrangements; however, my bubble burst all too soon.

"Sorry," she said. "There's no way we'll be able to capture all of that on film; not with the seven white doves being released. We just don't have the space to allow for such a wide shot."

I reported to the guest, and he was a little disappointed, but then he decided that releasing them in front of a fountain on Las Vegas Boulevard would do just as well.

"Maybe we should call the Las Vegas SPCA," a staffer said on overhearing our planning. She was an avid animal lover and worked at a local animal shelter. Her foresight regarding these precautions was greatly appreciated. After all, we didn't want to break any laws or harm any animals, or do anything that might bring the wrath of animal rights activists down on any of us, either. However, her foresight also put a quick end to the planned grandiosity.

"The hotel will be responsible for the welfare of the birds," they told us, "and in all likelihood, due to summer Vegas temperatures, the seven doves will fly around and eventually succumb to heat exhaustion. Knowledge of this could mean fines and bad publicity for the hotel."

Since none of us felt capable of trapping seven doves that had been released on Las Vegas Boulevard, and since we were equally reluctant to watch them crash and burn and then have to answer to the SPCA, the guest had to make his proposal without the doves.

It was still beautiful and memorable, and the guest's girlfriend was moved to tears. In retrospect, however, perhaps we could have made all of his vision a reality. We could have most likely found a magician headlining on the Strip who could have solved our quandary, as well as safely rounding up the doves in a puff of smoke.

• • •

There are around twenty thousand conventions held in Las Vegas every year, and when those who run international companies settle on Las Vegas for their conventions, the pressure is on. We concierges know that there are many places conventions can be held, but when it comes to inspiring employees and showing them how important they are to the company, three rules supersede all others in planning that convention: location, location, location.

The Vice President of Sales of a huge international company had booked our hotel for their marketing and sales convention. His first words to me were, "I know it is Vegas, and I know that anything can happen in Vegas."

I heard the challenge in his voice already, and I straightened my posture as a sign that I was ready, willing, and able to take on any request he could throw my way.

"We have a sales presentation tomorrow in the conference center. What I need from you is a yellow dinosaur costume. It's very important that it be yellow," he told me. "No green, no purple. Yellow."

Sure, I expected a strange request, but I was not prepared for this! This man was well over six feet tall, and I was trying to think of where in the world I would find a specifically yellow dinosaur costume. Oh, and did I mention that it was already Saturday night, and we were nowhere near the Halloween season? And I needed it *the next day!* My hopes of finding one were not very high, to say the least.

Still, I smiled at the towering guest and said, "I'll check into it and see what I can find, and I'll give your room a call as soon as I find something."

I called all the local party stores and costume rental stores, but most of them were already closed. I was going through the entire listing in the Yellow Pages alphabetically, and each time I actually got through to someone, the request was denied. I began to wrack my brain for other options. *Do schools have costume departments? But how would I get in touch with them on a Saturday night? What about some theaters around?* Finally, I found a costume store that was open, and they just happened to have a purple dinosaur costume that was for a tall person!

"It's almost perfect," I said. "The guest is quite tall, so that will work well. But it's purple," I remarked. "The guest was very adamant that it be yellow."

"Have no fear," the owner told me. "I can have it dyed yellow and delivered to you first thing tomorrow."

I was ecstatic, considering I didn't believe it could be done. The guest was over the moon as well. After delivering the costume, I couldn't help but sit back a moment, smile, and agree with the guest's earlier statement: "Anything can happen in Vegas!"

•   •   •

A concierge at an international hotel is accustomed to making special accommodations for guests of various cultures and religions. During Passover, for example, it is not uncommon for us to go out of our way for our Jewish guests.

Among some of my most memorable guests are a pair of lifelong friends—two guys from New York who are co-presidents of the company they founded. They're the most charming guys you could ever meet, and a stay at our hotel quickly became a Passover tradition for them. Although they arrived each year with their families in tow, their big thing was to try and surpass each other with some sort of elaborate practical joke.

I distinctly remember one of them approaching me shortly after they checked in one year.

"I need a camel," Max whispered dramatically to me.

To be sure of his specific desire, I replied, "A cigarette or a real camel?"

Max rolled his eyes at me, and I could almost hear him asking me what he would do with a cigarette. For him and his target, joking was a serious business.

"A camel," he spat. "An honest-to-goodness, Lawrence of Arabia, real live camel."

No shock showed on my face. After all, I had history with these two. I knew that Max and Sam pulled out all the stops when it came to their practical joking; Vegas was the perfect setting to do it, and I was the perfect concierge to help make it all happen.

"So, can you get me a camel?" he asked.

"I'm on it," I assured him.

"I don't need to tell you to keep it confidential, do I?" he posed, to which I shook my head.

For some reason, my mind began moving away from thinking this was part of a practical joke. In fact, I began wondering if this camel had something to do with one of the more obscure Jewish traditions that I hadn't known about. It was Passover, I reminded myself. Perhaps he needed the camel for religious reasons. I called everywhere I could think of and finally found someone close to Las Vegas willing to rent a couple of camels. The camels were delivered that night, and when they arrived, I went and quietly got Max.

The two of us walked out in front of the hotel, and there they were: a pair of real live camels with two fellows in Bedouin outfits. Max took one look at them and doubled over laughing.

"Oh! Oh, this is perfect," he gushed, and I think he actually wiped a tear from his eyes. "Follow me!"

Max and I took the two Bedouin guys with their animals and parked them outside the villa where Max's friend Sam was staying.

Max paid the guys half of the agreed-upon fee, and then, believe it or not, they camped out all night — Max included — in order to be there when Sam opened his door in the morning.

When Sam prepared to step out of his villa to join the rest of the gang for their rendezvous, he practically jumped out of his skin when he saw a pair of camels preening and spitting at him, accompanied by a couple of Bedouins just beyond his door. Very quickly though, Sam caught on to the joke, and he keeled over in laughter with his friend. The two pranksters thought this was the most hilarious thing they'd ever done to each other.

The Bedouin guys had caught the infectious frivolity of Sam and Max, and before they departed, they convinced Max and Sam to sit on the camels for a photo opp. As soon as the two pranksters climbed up on the camels and began posing for the pictures, one of the Bedouin guys clicked his tongue, which signaled for the camels to rear themselves on their hind legs. Max and Sam did what any other red-blooded American would do: they held on tightly and begged the trainers to stop. Then, having collected their wits about them, they asked the trainers if they could take a short jaunt around one of the holes on the golf course.

It was a sight to behold as the Bedouins traipsed around one of the holes with the camels. Serious golfers stopped to point, amazed at the sight of Sam and Max.

In the end, the duo was so relieved to finally be off the camels, they put their arms around each other and started heading back to their villas.

"Not so fast," I said as I headed them off at the pass. I fixed my glare on them. "Who's going to clean up all this camel dung?"

They each pointed at the other and feigned innocence at first. But I knew that they knew it had to be them, and sure enough, it was. The whole thing ended with these two company presidents shoveling piles – and I do mean piles – of camel dung while the players on the golf course got more entertainment than any game of golf they'd ever played in their lives. Since then, Sam and Max still come to our hotel every year with their families for Passover, but after the camel prank, they have decided that there is no topping that one.

• • •

When guests come to Vegas to celebrate their birthdays, they expect to pull out all the stops. One guest called to discuss with me her upcoming fiftieth birthday celebration, and she wanted it to be a blow-out . . . quite literally.

"I'm coming to Vegas with a group of my girlfriends," she told me. "It's a fiftieth birthday celebration that's been in the making for years, so I want it to live up to all my hopes and dreams," she told me.

"I can promise you that I'll do my best," I said with pride. I'd had success with many birthdays on the grandest of scales, not to mention anniversaries, wedding proposals, and weddings themselves.

"It's important to me that the weekend should not be just about me, even though it is my birthday," she informed me. "I want my guests to be treated extra special. They're paying a lot of money and taking a lot of time off to come and celebrate with me, and I want them to know how much it means to me."

"What did you have in mind?" I asked her.

She told me she'd like a limo to pick them up at the airport, complete with champagne for the ride and then champagne and chocolate-covered strawberries in the suite when they arrived. She proceeded with her list as I took notes. None of her requests was extraordinary that I could see. After we'd handled the mundane dinner reservations and show tickets... then she threw the curve ball at me.

"Ok, so back to the arrival at the airport," she said to me. "I'd like to have a Frank Sinatra or Dean Martin-style singer greet us at the airport to sing to us as we wait for and collect our luggage."

"Like a lounge-singer of sorts?" I asked, the list of requests sounding more intriguing to me now.

"Exactly. Just to sing, though. I don't expect him to carry our luggage or anything. And I have a few songs I'd actually like for him to include. I can email them to you, if you'd like."

"Great," I said, and I rattled off my email address to her.

"Is there anything else you'd like upon your arrival?" I asked.

I could practically hear the inspiration strike before she began giggling and then came out with her new request.

"Ooh, yes! Perfect! I want a blow-up doll in each of my friends' beds as a joke – inflated and ready to go, if you know what I mean."

Now, this was not my first request for a blow-up doll to be placed in a guest's room, but I was getting light-headed merely thinking about how much air that was going to take for me to inflate two or three of those things by myself. I'd have to come up with some sort of plan.

I took my lunch hour and headed to the nearest adult superstore and purchased the dolls and worked up my nerve to ask for some assistance with blowing up the toys.

"We can do that here," the guy told me. "This would be a lot of blowing for you to do all by yourself."

Once he'd inflated the dolls, however, I realized the new problem I'd just created for myself: I would have to carry the dolls all the way back to the hotel, through the crowded lobby, and up to the suite—fully inflated and 'ready for action,' so to speak!

Swallowing my pride, I began the walk back to the hotel. Perhaps the funniest aspect of the whole situation was the fact that I got far fewer looks and glances than I was anticipating. Maybe the sight of a concierge carrying a few full-sized blow-up dolls down the Strip and into the lobby of a Vegas hotel was not as 'out of the ordinary' as I'd expected.

And I'm happy to report that the guest's birthday was exactly the "blow-out" she'd dreamed of . . . and more.

• • •

I think a concierge is born with a special gene that almost forces us to be ready to help, no matter the request. I know I have found myself bending over backwards before I really even think about what guests are asking me for. For example, there was the guest who came to the hotel as part of a business convention who, while his peers were out racing ATVs in the desert and gambling on the

Strip, begged me for a tour of the hotel trash facilities (complete with a question/answer period at the end).

There was also the guest who was in the process of moving to a small island in the South Pacific and enlisted my help to purchase two satellite phones at $25,000 dollars each. Turns out it's not as easy as one would expect, and there's a lot of government red tape to get through, and I'm sure my friends I called on for help thought I was helping either a drug kingpin or a mafia boss.

And then there was the wife who was bringing her husband to Vegas for their anniversary.

"He loved that movie *The Hangover*," she told me, "and he's been wanting to visit Vegas ever since. Do you think you could have a white tiger—line in the movie—put in the bathroom so that it scares him to death when he opens the door?"

That one hadn't taken much thinking; I knew her request was impossible, but I immediately convinced her to have an extremely large stuffed white tiger instead and had it waiting for him as a welcome wagon of sorts. I can only imagine the look on his face when he saw it, and when he heard that his wife had at first wanted to put a real tiger in there!

I even had a guest call down to my desk and ask if I could find some breast milk for her, and without even batting an eye, my first thought was, "Now who do I know who's lactating?"

That's what I mean when I say that a concierge is born to serve, and especially after serving for years in a city like Las Vegas, our sense of reality and the requests therein becomes a little warped. So when a comedy troupe asked me to find them a straitjacket, I really thought nothing of it at first.

This was a very avant garde comedy troupe who specialized in using magic and special effects for quite the outrageous comedic experience. They had come to perform for a convention party in one of the ballrooms, and I had been quite impressed with their preparations for the show. Suddenly, the preparations halted. Everything had been in perfect order, all in readiness until they realized that one of their props was missing: a straitjacket.

As I said before, I wasn't too concerned when one of the performers approached me in a panic, requesting my help in procuring a straitjacket. After all, I've had stranger requests, and this is Vegas, after all—a town known for its many and varied shows. Surely the home of Siegfried and Roy would have extra straitjackets at its disposal!

Right?

Wrong.

In fact, straitjackets, having been deemed inhumane by the medical field, hadn't been used for almost two decades, making it a lot less likely that someone might have one lying around somewhere. Still, it was an important part of their act, and it was up to me and my staff to procure one before curtain time. Which meant only one thing: it was time to panic.

Before the anxiety completely conquered my wits, however, a thought struck me.

"Let's call the larger hospitals in the area," I suggested. I knew that hospitals had little areas near the ER. I also knew that there were special procedures for dealing with those patients who couldn't be controlled by conventional means—maybe those with drug and alcohol abuse or those who were exhibiting a psychosis of one sort or another.

"Perhaps some of them have straitjackets for extreme cases," I thought, and I pictured the movie *Silence of the Lambs* when Hannibal Lecter was being transported, how they had wrapped him in a straitjacket for fear he would eat one of the guards.

I had a friend who worked at one of the larger hospitals in Vegas, and I decided to call him.

"We don't use straitjackets anymore," he informed me, "but I'll take a look. Perhaps in a storage closet or something where we keep the outdated equipment."

It took a bit of time, and he had to go to old forgotten storage rooms in a wing of the hospital that they didn't use anymore, but in some back room with dusty equipment, sure enough, he found a straitjacket.

"You're not going to believe this!" he said when he called me up, and I sent a runner over to him to retrieve the last straitjacket in Las Vegas. And none too soon! We had the prop on the table twenty-five minutes before the curtain went up!

This entire scenario had given us all a new take on the term "wardrobe malfunction", though that's the kind of jacket I never want to see hanging in my closet.

• • •

Often, as a concierge, I'm helping guests in ways I can't even imagine. For example, I had this guest approach me one day and, before even introducing himself, he slapped down a crisp $100 bill on my desk.

"Tennis, dinner, a show," he exclaimed in a thick Russian accent. "I need you to set me up today with the works."

I smiled and proceeded to ask questions about his preferences as I lined up the requested tickets.

Then, every day thereafter, it was the same drill. He showed up at my desk, produced a $100 bill, and gave me the requests for the day. None of them were too difficult; all his requests were pretty ordinary and easy to accommodate.

Finally, on the fifth and final day of his stay at the hotel, he showed up, slapped the $100 dollar bill down, and announced in a booming voice, "I have something a little more difficult in mind for the grand finale today."

My mind raced through many options, and given his accent, I wasn't sure what to expect.

He leaned in and whispered secretively, "I need a contractor."

Now, maybe I was being stereotypical, and maybe I've seen too many James Bonds movies, but immediately, I wondered where in the world I would find a hit man for this guy. My lips began moving, but I could tell there was no sound coming from them. I didn't know what words to even say!

The guest winked at me and began a low laugh. "Uh-huh. I got you," he said. "I told you it would be a tough one. You've gotten away with easy, silly little requests all week. Now this will show me what you're truly made of."

"But . . . I . . ." I couldn't even think of how to tell this man that I had no idea how to go about finding a contract killer for him, and to tell the truth, I wasn't sure I wanted to make him angry with me.

"Come on," he interrupted, "surely you can find out who the contractor was on this great hotel. Isn't that the best place to start?"

I stared at him, my mouth slightly agape. So, he wanted to hire a *contractor*, a builder.

"I own land in Sochi, Russia, the town where they will be holding the 2014 Winter Olympics. Your hotel here in Las Vegas is so beautiful, I would like to hire the same people to build my hotel. I have the plans and everything else done. I just need a contractor to get the ball rolling. Russian laborers with this talent? Hard to find sometimes."

By the time my guest had left the next day, I had managed to set up a conference call with a Boston company for the following week in Hawaii, where the guest was headed next. In the end, the deal did not go through, but my guest was very thankful nonetheless. I was just happy to have helped him . . . and glad I could put to rest all those images of *From Russia with Love*.

•   •   •

It's easy for things to get lost in translation, and with international accents coloring the English language, it is easy to mistake—or think you have mistaken—what a guest asks for. A Japanese couple came to me with a request one day that I was certain I'd misheard.

"I'm sorry," I said kindly. "What is it that you need?"

When he repeated himself, I realized I had NOT misheard. It was exactly what I'd feared he'd said.

"I need bull testicles."

I plastered a big smile on my face, hoping — praying — for the hidden cameras to come out soon so that I wouldn't embarrass myself too much, but when he stood before me with a hopeful look in his eye, his jaw set and determined, I kissed those hopes goodbye and felt the wide-eyed alarm.

"Okay," I finally said, but I couldn't bring myself to move more than my blinking eyes.

"Do you know of a place to get them?" he asked.

I could be honest here. "No," I said, "but I will research it for you most certainly and find exactly what you wish for."

"They are a delicacy in Japan," he informed me, and I had to admit I felt myself sag a little in relief. "I want to ship them to a family friend at home, and I would greatly appreciate your help."

I nodded, very business-like, and promised to get right on the task. However, when I called a few specialty and ethnic delis to make my inquiry, you can imagine the responses I received.

It suddenly occurred to me that I was looking in the wrong places. A deli wasn't going to be the best option, so I tried a few butchers, but I got the same response. Finally, one of them suggested a rather large ranch in California, not too far away.

"I know where it is," I answered, feeling my hopes lift.

"They've got quite a bull population," the butcher told me.

"And where there are bulls, there must be testicles," I said.

So, I called them immediately and found out that they did in fact have the testicles we needed.

My guests were thrilled when I told them that I'd found them. So then, I set about the task of placing the order and arranging the shipping. When it was all said and done, the Japanese couple paid about eight thousand dollars for the testicles and an additional three thousand in shipping.

For days, my co-workers asked questions:

"Just how big were those testicles?"

"Did you try this delicacy?"

"How do they prepare it?"

I quickly informed them that I had not seen them or sampled them, but that I could provide them with the contact information of the ranch if they were so curious about size and taste.

And that's no bull.

•  •  •

Every now and then, something goes missing or gets stolen at the hotel. It's inevitable with so many guests coming and going, and the drinks flowing. We've had several occasions when guests have invited people back to their rooms for an impromptu party, and half of those in attendance are perfect strangers to the guest.

One morning, a guest called me in quite a state. Someone had stolen his wallet.

My heart went out to him. "I'm so sorry, sir," I said. "Let me transfer you to security."

"No, no," he interrupted me quickly. "Wait just a second before you do that. See, it's a bit of an odd situation," he continued. "I know who did it."

"Excuse me?"

"I know who stole my wallet," he clarified.

"Well, I guess that's a little bit of good news," I said a bit more cheerily. "Would you like to file a police report, then?"

"No!" the man said quickly.

I was trying to make sense of all of this. How was I going to be able to help if he knew the thief but didn't want me to put him in touch with the police? I was beginning to question my role in this request. Then a possibility dawned on me.

"Oh," I said slowly. "Was your wallet taken by one of your friends?"

"No. It wasn't a friend," the guest replied.

I'm usually a very patient person—you have to be in this job— but my patience was beginning to wane, and he wasn't giving me much information. Just as I was about to ask him how I could help him with his situation, he finally got to the point.

"The truth is, I got a hooker last night," he said. "She stole my wallet, but I don't know how to get in touch with her."

I was certain this was not the first guest to bring a prostitute into the hotel. Not that they always checked them in at the front desk, but . . . well, you just know these things, and it's Vegas after all. It was, however, the first time I'd had a guest openly admit to it ... and call to report that his overnight guest had stolen from him.

"Please," he began begging, "can you help me track her down? I've got to get my wallet back."

There was a part of me that felt very sorry for the man, but then I wondered if he had a girlfriend or wife, and a part of me felt less sorry for him then. Still, there were rules in place for situations like this for a reason—which meant that he wasn't the first to have suffered at the hands of a lady of the night.

Finally, I said, "I'm so sorry, sir. There's no way I can help you, though. We're not permitted to address those kinds of issues. I'm sure you understand."

Without so much as a "thank you", the man hung up, which made me feel even less sorry for him. In a way, he'd done some gambling of a different kind that night, and much to his chagrin, he'd made what he thought was a small bet, but lost it all in the end.

That's the game sometimes.

# Money Matters

## Ante Up

Money can allow people to fulfill their strangest desires, and in a Las Vegas hotel, this often requires the help of a concierge. The result can mean that those concierges find themselves in hilarious, uncomfortable, or fascinating situations. Most of all, guests with tons of money and odd requests make for memories that are not easily forgotten.

For those of us who aren't billionaires, life happens very differently. As a concierge, though, it's always nice to be able to live vicariously for a bit when these guests frequent my hotel. There are a lot of unique experiences in this business, and add an insanely rich guest into the mix, and the job takes an even more interesting twist. At the beginning of my career, I worked at a smaller boutique hotel. One thing that I loved about it was that there was the opportunity for a more intimate rapport with guests. I'll never forget one experience with a woman from Texas. She was the poster child for the idea that "Everything's bigger in Texas."

Her name was Dixie, and she had some of the biggest hair I'd ever seen—long blonde curls that ran the length of her shoulders with extra volume she piled on top. She also had a big voice—you could always tell when she was coming into the lobby; she greeted everyone along the hallways, and when she entered from her day or night on the town, the lobby filled with the sound of her exclamation. Dixie most assuredly had the biggest personality I had encountered at that time in my career. Everyone was "darlin'" in her book, and she had a magnetism that drew people to her when she entered the room. Oh, make no mistake: Dixie was good-looking, but she exuded a confidence and sense of grandeur that compelled people towards her.

It was on Dixie's last day with us that she submitted a request to me. She was going to go ahead and check out, though her plane didn't leave until seven that evening.

"There's just this one thing that's been plaguing me, and I thought perhaps you could help me with it," she said.

Then she launched into a detailed story about a pair of gold Manolo Blahnik shoes she'd encountered on a previous visit to New York.

"I can't get these shoes out of my head," Dixie drawled. "I'd love it if you could help me find a place that might have a pair here in Vegas before I have to go back to Texas. Do you think that's possible, darlin'?"

I beamed a toothy grin at her. How could anyone say "no" to that?

I immediately got to work, searching the internet and calling boutiques and shops. I knew what it was like to be haunted by the perfect pair of shoes, so I was pulling out all the stops to help this sweet lady, but it was proving to be a bit more difficult than I first anticipated.

"We have a pair of gold Jimmy Choos a lot like that," one attendant told me, but I wouldn't settle.

"I have a sapphire blue, diamond-studded Manolo Blahnik heel that I think she'll like," another said, but I just thanked them kindly and said I'd keep looking.

Eventually, I got in touch with a local merchant who had one pair of the exact shoes I needed, and it was just her size!

"Perfect! I'll take it!" I said excitedly.

"The total will be eight-hundred thirty-six dollars and twelve cents," he replied. "Will you be putting this on your Visa?"

My heart raced and dropped at the same time. Over eight hundred bucks for a pair of shoes?! Who were these people who could afford this? And why couldn't I be one of them?

"Not my Visa," I said to him, "but let me explain my story." I told the store manager the story and emphasized how badly my guest was wanting these shoes. "She's having dinner at the hotel bar right now," I informed them. "It would be so great if we could get them over here in less than forty-five minutes. She'll be leaving to catch a plane back to Texas then."

I held my breath, already thinking through my next line of attack; I had forty-five minutes left to get those shoes, and I wasn't going to take no for an answer.

"I'll do better than that," the manager said. "I'll bring them over and surprise her at her table. Will you be around to point her out?"

My Texas Cinderella was enjoying the last sips of her wine when the store manager arrived with her shoes. I introduced the two of them; Dixie eyed the bag suspiciously, and then the manager dropped to his knees, and palmed the lady's shoe in his hand.

"May I?" he asked genteelly.

She nodded with anticipation, and when he placed the gold Manolo Blahnik onto her foot, Dixie squealed with delight, causing all the other diners in the restaurant to crane their necks towards the sound, of course.

"This is so wonderful!" she kept saying as she examined the shoes, turning her foot one way and then the other. "I can't believe you did this!"

She hugged me tightly. "I was just hoping for a store name, a phone number, where I could hopefully order them once I got home. But this?" Dixie reached forward and hugged the store manager. "Ya'll are just too kind! I feel like I'm in a fairytale!"

It was one of those perfect moments when everything had worked together to exceed the expectations of a guest. I smiled at her, reveling in her happiness.

I told her it was the least we could do for such a Texas darlin'.

• • •

Of course, there are always those who really want to live it up while they're in Las Vegas. Sometimes, though, the cost of living it up is more than one could ever imagine.

"I want the very best, and money is no object."

I've heard that phrase so many times in my line of work, whether it's the queen's treatment at the spa or the most elaborate wedding proposal ever, many guests will tell a concierge to think nothing of the cost. On some occasions, it becomes clear that the guest hasn't thought too much about the cost either!

Such was the case when a young guest strolled over to my desk many years ago, girlfriend in tow.

"Hey," he said. "I'd like to go on a cruise ... a private cruise for a week. On a yacht."

In my head, the dollars were already adding up, and I heard the 'cha-chings' of the charges accumulating.

"I must inform you, sir, that your request will be quite expensive," I replied, hesitantly.

"I don't care," he said. "I'll pay whatever it costs."

I nodded, and he asked me to call his room when I'd collected the information.

I spent the rest of the day making the calls, gathering information that he'd requested, but before I booked anything specific, I called his room.

"So, I found a few options for you," I told him. "It looks like the cheapest of your options to cruise for a week on a private yacht will run to about $3,000 per day," I told him.

"What?!"

I could almost feel the shock coming through the phone. He was incredulous. "I'd expected to pay that much for a whole week on board," he said.

"I'm sorry for the sticker-shock," I said to him. "It sounds to me that your price range is actually closer to a week on board a commercial cruise line."

He was silent for a few beats, and I wondered what I should do. In my mind red lights were flashing and warning signals were going off, and I could hear someone shouting, "Man overboard! Man overboard!"

"Would you like me to book the private yacht for you sir?" I asked tentatively, though I felt I knew the answer already.

The man declined vehemently.

I quickly learned that sometimes, "whatever it costs" is a bigger bite than some guests are prepared to chew!

•   •   •

Arranging luxurious stays for wealthy guests and their entourage is a big part of any Las Vegas concierge's job. However, I've learned that sometimes, in spite of the saying, what happens in Vegas doesn't always stay in Vegas. There have been times when what happened in Vegas did indeed follow guests home.

An Australian gentleman was staying at my hotel once, and he made it clear that he wanted "nothing but the best" for himself and his mates.

"I want everything top of the line," he informed me. "Never question cost, and if you're trying to decide between two items, go with the more expensive; it's usually worth it."

He had already booked our brand new forty-thousand-dollar-a-night suite and had requested a drum set, an electric guitar, and a bass guitar to be waiting for them in the suite when they arrived.

"I'd also like a humidor filled with Cuban cigars," he instructed.

"Cuban cigars are illegal, sir, but I will find a way to still get you some of the best cigars around."

Already, I had an idea taking shape. Word among the staff was that Geraldo, a young man who worked in the kitchen, was Cuban and could roll the most beautiful cigars. I tracked him down, offered him the task, and he performed beautifully. This also gave me the opportunity to tell the Australian gentleman that he had hand-rolled Cuban-style cigars of the best tobacco, an exclusive gift he greatly appreciated.

He also flew in his own personal stylist from New York who, armed with the measurements of each soon-to-arrive guest, filled the suite's closets with the latest in top-name fashions. (I must admit that I was envious of the threads these guys were accumulating as I saw the wardrobes brought in the day before the visit.) Since money was no object, the Australian guest paid for everyone's first-class round trip airfare—including the stylist's—and hotel stay in addition to all their meals at five-star restaurants. On top of that, the stylist still charged him an outrageous fee for her work, but when you have money like he obviously did, I guess it all seems worth it.

For three days straight, these five Australians lived the high life. They took helicopter tours of the city and the desert; they sat VIP at shows on the Strip complete with meet-and-greets with the casts. They also celebrated one of the group's birthday at a local spa at sunset, with cake and only the best champagne.

Of course, we have guests who spare no expense, so I thought nothing of all of this until several months later. I happened to read in a magazine that the very same Australian magnate had been arrested Down Under. The crime? Embezzling millions of dollars.

My eyes nearly popped out of my head as I recalled all the tabs he'd run up, the total cost of all he'd done in Vegas. Turned out he was playing with house money, and when you do that, "The house always wins."

• • •

Sometimes with guests, you just don't know what you're getting. I remember one guest in particular who inadvertently taught me not to judge a book by its cover. When he approached my desk, everything about this guest screamed, "Eccentric!"

He wore a faded Harley-Davidson t-shirt with shorts, socks that were pulled up to his knees and peeking out over the top of his black leather biker boots. His beard was shaved in odd, angular edges and hid his facial features and his eyes. Upon seeing him, my first thought was that he was quite a character!

"Good afternoon, sir. Are you checking in?" I asked, not entirely sure he was staying at this hotel that was known for being high-dollar.

"I checked in yesterday," he informed me. "But today is my girlfriend's birthday."

I smiled and nodded. "I want to take her to the nicest restaurant you know of. Money is no object. I don't care what it costs."

As I've said, those familiar words always inspire a sense of dread, as I wonder if the guest really knows what that might mean. The feeling of dread began to spread as I took in the sight of the guest and tried to visualize him in the nicest restaurant I knew of. He didn't fit the picture, and I wondered if he knew what he was asking. The best place I knew of could cost in the thousands, and that's not including a bottle or two of good wine or champagne.

However, as a concierge it's my duty to do as requested, not to pass judgment.

"Absolutely," I replied. "How about if I give you a list of the best places, and you tell me which one you think would be most appealing to her? Then, I'll make the reservations for you for this evening."

He liked the idea, and we settled on a nearby four-diamond restaurant complete with black-tie service. It boasted a beautiful upscale atmosphere, delicious food, elegance—basically perfection. The whole time, though — I have to admit — I was feeling bad about the possibility of canceling later when the guest found out exactly what he'd gotten himself into.

The reservations made, he excused himself to his room to prepare for the evening. A few minutes later, I received a phone call from a salesman with a local luxury car dealership.

"I'm calling to confirm a delivery," he said. "One Ferrari and an Aston Martin for a Mr. Darcy."

I'm a little ashamed to say that my jaw dropped open, and as I was picking it up off the floor, I took a second to Google my eccentric guest's name.

There he was – a famous collector who regularly spends millions of dollars on luxury vehicles. In fact, according to Wikipedia, he had more than one hundred of these vehicles in his collection at present.

The vision of him in his faded Harley-Davidson t-shirt and high white socks, weird beard and stooped shoulders contrasted with the picture of him on Wikipedia. He was shaved cleaner, standing erect, and wearing a William Fioravanti suit — the same one he appeared wearing later before leaving for his girlfriend's birthday dinner.

When the cars were delivered, Mr. Darcy chose the Aston Martin, and drove his girlfriend to dinner at that gorgeous restaurant. I'm still trying to decide who was more impressed, me or the girlfriend!

• • •

Usually, we see female guests arrive for their stays with twice to three times the luggage of your typical male guest. Of course, I understand this: a girl needs her options when spending some time on the Strip. But one male guest I encountered finally beat all luggage records and still holds the title.

A wealthy Saudi guest arrived at our Las Vegas hotel via his private jet for less than a week in Las Vegas. I am not exaggerating when I say he did not pack lightly, but one of the reasons for his trip was to do some shopping, too.

After a wonderful stay (his words) and several days' worth of spending, he prepared to leave and presented us with a unique situation: with the luggage he'd brought with him and the things he'd ended up purchasing during his stay, this man had ninety-eight suitcases to take home! Ninety-eight! And that wasn't counting any oversized items that he'd purchased and had shipped directly to his home in Saudi Arabia.

Of course, we had nowhere near the manpower to help him with all of his bags; nor did we have the fleet to transport all of his "baggage" to the airport. What we finally did was rent a large, specially made luggage tube to transport his suitcases from the hotel back to the airport and to his private jet.

To this day, this still stands as the record for the highest number of bags attached to a single Las Vegas visitor.

In fact, in all my years as a concierge, I've never seen a shopping-addicted wife, a touring musician, or a fashion-conscious celebrity come even close to beating our Middle Eastern VIP and his harem of suitcases.

•   •   •

Eccentric guests are always a bit of a challenge—though they make for some interesting experiences and stories.  But if they happen to be eccentric *billionaire* guests, the challenge reaches another level altogether.  I have found myself complying with unconventional requests, including hiring acrobats for the weekend as well as traipsing to an infamous department store every single day to purchase brand new underwear. Why? Because I had a particular male guest who never wore the same underwear twice! I thought this was going to be the strangest or most surprising thing about this guest, but I was wrong.

It turned out that this eccentric guest was in Las Vegas mainly because he was interested in a particular piece of land for some cattle he'd recently purchased.  He had to stay in Vegas because there were no hotels in the area of the land he was inspecting, but this meant that he needed a flight from Vegas out to the land. There was one major problem my guest had with the commuter planes that routinely went to the target area: no bathrooms on board. So, one day, he approached me and said, "I need you to find me a plane."

"What type of plane?" I asked.

At first he replied, "I don't care," and then he leaned in a little closer and added, "as long as there's a bathroom on it." Then he thought for a few seconds and amended himself. "I think it needs to be a jet."

"Okay, I'll look into chartering a jet," I told him with a smile.

His hand went up immediately as he began to shake his head. "No, no, no. I don't want to charter it. I'm going to buy the plane," the guest replied.

I'd never had a request quite like this one before, so I was quite taken aback, but I told the guest I'd look into it. I began calling around the private airport and asking questions. I said that I didn't know how serious the guest was, but that I needed to know whether there were any private jets for sale. With a bathroom.

*Surely he's pulling my leg*, I thought. Still, I proceeded in my efforts to fulfill his request just in case he wasn't.

About two hours later, I finally found myself in touch with an agent at the private airport. He agreed to come to the hotel and meet with my guest to discuss a jet that was for sale. I snuck glances over to the two men as they met in the lobby, and when I finally saw them shake hands, smiles wide across their faces, I knew I had been wrong to doubt my guest. He strode over later to thank me for my help.

"You're amazing!" he remarked.

"I'm amazed," I corrected. "I've never been a part of a deal to purchase a private jet. With or without a bathroom."

He continued to smile. "The best part about it is that I got it for a steal—only a couple million dollars!"

*Steal indeed*, I thought, shaking my head at the idea.

Obviously, he had not been kidding about buying his own private jet. As he left the hotel on his way to look at the land he was interested in purchasing, I couldn't help but allow myself a fleeting thought: I hoped that after all that, he formed a better attachment to the jet than he did his undies. If not, life could get even more expensive than he'd ever imagined.

• • •

Every guest who comes into our hotels comes with specific nuances and needs. Just look at the Saudi with all of his luggage, the woman with her pampered pooch, and the man who was allergic to almost everything. I'll never forget the time a Texas oil billionaire stayed with us. He brought with him a few bodyguards. His main bodyguard was not only responsible for the oil tycoon's safety, but he was also responsible for carrying around a leather bag stuffed full of one-hundred dollar bills.

I got to see a different side of this guest, as he invited me to accompany him and his friends to a well-known Las Vegas nightclub for a birthday party. Eager to see this new nightclub, I prepared myself carefully, putting on my best dress and high heels.

What I wasn't prepared for, however, was how unreserved the oil tycoon was with his money. He tipped everyone! He tipped the security guards, the servers, the hosts – anyone who had any kind of contact with us, and when I say "tipped", I mean several hundred-dollar bills at a time. He bought $5,000 bottles of champagne like they were mere two-bit souvenirs. My eyes nearly fell out of my head at how much money this man was handing out.

Of course I knew he had money. He'd booked the most expensive suites in the hotel, complete with private infinity pools, massage rooms, etc. But the way he simply handed money out during this night on the town was flabbergasting.

When we left the nightclub, he indicated that the night wasn't over.

"There's entertainment in my suite back at the hotel," he mentioned to me. He was chuckling a little, and of course, this left me wondering what in the world this surprise entertainment was. "I hope you'll come check it out," he invited.

Of course I was curious—and a little worried, I must confess. When I returned to the hotel, he invited a few other staffers to come up to his suite, and so a couple of colleagues and I headed up to see what was going on.

When we got there, a small crowd had already gathered and were mingling, eating and drinking, mainly in the bedroom. As I approached the room, my anxiety was building with each step.

On the bed were two little people, smacking each other as hard as they could with pillows that were almost the same size they were. The little fellas were bare-chested and wore white cotton pants much like pajamas as they whirled and grunted and slammed each other with all their tiny might.

The room was filled with the guest's friends, who were watching the fight with amusement and placing bets on the outcome.

Several thoughts were flashing through my head. First, I was relieved that it wasn't some crazy, kinky sex show (which had been my first thought, I had to admit), but secondly, I found myself wondering how this guest had managed to find these little people, and then what he had said to them to get them to do this. How do you approach it? And what does it pay?

"Hi! I'm so-and-so, and I'll pay you such-and-such hundred dollars if you'll come to my hotel room and have a good, old-fashioned pillow fight in front of a few of my friends."

I realized at that moment that if you have enough money, amusing yourself is never a problem. After a while, I politely thanked the guest for a memorable evening, and then excused myself from the room. As I was leaving his suite, my head was absolutely spinning. Doing quick math and not counting the entertainment I'd just witnessed, I knew that the man's nightclub excursion had cost at the very least $125,000. I just kept thinking that it would take me almost three years of working and saving every single dollar to make the amount of money that my guest had handed out in the course of a few hours! But there was one thing I felt good about: I had no idea how much he'd paid the little people to pillow fight, but based on all I had witnessed myself, I have a feeling they made out like tiny bandits.

# Famous Faces

## Paying the Runner

One of the coolest things about
being a concierge in Vegas
is having the opportunity to
meet some of the most famous
people in the world. Sometimes,
it can be awkward or funny,
because as a concierge, you're
allowed just a few steps into
these people's private worlds.
Famous people often make
the most outlandish requests
of a concierge, and as you're
about to see, the results can
end up miraculous, or very
uncomfortable.

There are two things the general public may not know about a certain Motown crooner, a blind "wonder" of a musician. The first is that he never books his Vegas hotel rooms in advance, and the other is that he has a phenomenal memory. It was a Valentine's Day weekend; therefore, our hotel was packed. I received a phone call from a man who identified himself as the bodyguard of this "Wonder"ful musician.

"We're en route to your hotel, and we're going to need a two-bedroom suite," he said. He hung up before I had an opportunity to say anything.

At first I thought, *Is this guy for real, or am I the butt of some practical joke, here?* Still, I didn't want to take any chances, so I sped over to the front desk and asked if we had any two-bedroom suites.

A laugh was what I got in response at first. "Are you kidding me?" the attendant quipped. "Do you *know* what weekend this is?"

"Okay, okay, dumb question," I conceded. "How about any reservations that are vacant at the moment?"

Though his first instinct was to glare at me, he took a long, slow breath and said he'd check. Thankfully, we had some open, and I clapped my hands in response.

"Look, I have someone coming in, and we *cannot* turn him away. I'll personally walk the previous guest to another hotel, but this musician is coming, and we're going to check him into this suite."

I went out front to wait for his arrival, and after about half an hour, a limousine pulled in and the legend stepped out. I had met this music icon one other time, fifteen years earlier at another hotel in Petaluma, California. All those years ago, after I had introduced myself and welcomed him, I asked if he was in town for a special occasion. His quick answer was, "I'm here to pet a luma, and if you can't pet a luma, what can you pet?"

As I watched him step out of the limo in Vegas, I chuckled at the memory. Then, I walked over and introduced myself again. Since he was blind, I carefully and lightly took his hand so as not to startle him, and I said, "I had the pleasure of meeting you about fifteen years ago at another hotel."

He replied, "Yes. I remember. I was doing a concert in Petaluma, and I joked that if you can't pet a luma, what could you pet?" I was impressed! There are times when I struggle to remember a guest's face and name after a long hiatus from them, but I seriously doubted I could remember someone just by the sound of his or her voice! I was blown away that he had remembered me after all that time and all the people he had met. I took him to his suite and made sure he was comfortable. His bodyguard told me that they'd like to come down in about an hour for dinner if I could arrange it.

It just so happened that we had a piano player providing the dinner music that night, and my musical guest seemed to be enjoying the melody. His head swayed back and forth in time to the music, and he smiled that million-dollar smile that was a song all its own.

After his dinner, my guest said to me, "Would that happen to be Carlos P. playing the piano?"

Carlos had been our regular pianist for years, and I replied in the affirmative.

"Would you go over and ask if I could join him on the piano?" my guest asked me. "Please tell him who I am and remind him that he and I played a concert together in Germany."

I knew that if I were Carlos, I'd be honored, so I wasted no time in repeating the message to him. He, of course, was thrilled and told me to bring our special guest over at once.

"I haven't seen him since Germany, one of the highlights of my career by far!"

I guided my guest over toward the piano. The dining room was absolutely loaded with lovers celebrating Valentine's Day, and when our guest sat down at the piano, suddenly, there was a thundering applause and diners were whistling and shouting. The other guests were completely enamored, and our musician played sweet love songs with Carlos for about an hour and a half. I'd be willing to bet there wasn't one guest who moved during that impromptu, private concert for fear of missing one second. For many of us, it was a most memorable Valentine's Day experience.

● ● ●

Vegas is not just a destination for tourists and conventions. Even Hollywood stars fall in love with Vegas and frequent the lavish hotels and casinos. In the early 1990s, a famous blue-eyed singer/actor had reached his seventy-seventh birthday. By that time in his life, he had experienced the ups and downs of a remarkable career, but he'd also established a reputation for having a volatile, two-sided personality. People close to him said that when he was nice, he was very nice, but when he got into a fit about someone or something, it could be very ugly. It was easy to understand, then, how he'd earned the nickname "Chairman of the Board" in addition to his more well-known and endearing moniker, "Old Blue Eyes."

At one visit to our hotel, as The Chairman was getting ready to head back to his Vegas penthouse suite after a show, an elderly woman started walking alongside him and his phalanx of bodyguards. When the group got to the elevators, one of the bodyguards brushed her aside to open the door for his boss.

That, however, did not sit well with our guest of honor.

I watched in amazement as The Chairman pushed his bodyguard out of the way, took the elderly woman by the hand, and gently led her back to the elevator. He pressed the up button and made sure that she got safely onto the elevator. Then, he unleashed his anger on his bodyguard. Old Blue Eyes was a fairly wiry man, especially compared to the muscle-bound bodyguards who surrounded him. He stood at five feet, eight inches in height, nose to nose with the broad-shouldered protector while he gave him quite the tongue-lashing. Sternly, with poke after poke into the iron chest of the bodyguard, The Chairman instructed his employee that he would never treat a woman like that again.

The bodyguard hung his head like a scolded child and followed Old Blue Eyes into the elevator, a contrite look on his face.

On another occasion, The Chairman got wind that a pair of newlywed fans were coming to his show that night. During that twilight stage of his career, this iconic star was seeing a surge in his popularity. It was a veritable rebirth for him but with a completely new generation of fans. From stories I'd heard and what I'd witnessed myself, he seemed to get an extra big kick out of his younger fans, especially ones like these who professed to have all his albums but weren't even born when his career began.

Old Blue Eyes was endeared to the couple immediately, and he arranged for them to be seated in the front row with a complementary bottle of champagne. At the end of the show, he took his monogrammed handkerchief out of his pocket and gave it to them as a memento. As you might expect, the young couple couldn't stop raving the next day about the special treatment they had received.

But what I admire most about this entertainer was the time he came down to my desk at the hotel carrying the Las Vegas paper.

"Did you see this?" he asked me, pointing to the article on the front page I had indeed read that morning. The story was about a family with a disabled daughter whose customized van had been stolen. It was imperative they had it to transport her to doctor's appointments, therapy, and school.

"How can people do this? A classic Cadillac, sure; I get it, but why would you steal a specialized van for someone's kid?" He was beside himself, and I saw a flash of that legendary ire in his eyes.

"So I'm hoping you can do a little research for me and get me a few guys to talk to. I'm gonna buy this family a replacement."

And just like that, he did. Though he'd never met them or seen them before, we worked it out to be delivered to the family's home.

With ease, he made a decision on a van, wrote a check for just under $100,000, and insisted that his identity be kept secret. It was a kindness I will never forget, and one I suspect I'm not likely to see again anytime soon.

• • •

A professional football player came to me asking for help with a popular Las Vegas play.

"I'm flying my girlfriend into town this weekend, and I am planning to propose at the hotel."

I smiled. I love many aspects of my job, but helping with weddings and wedding proposals is a personal favorite of mine.

"I'm good at a lot of things," he boasted, "but I'm not exactly creative when it comes to being romantic. Can you please help me?"

I assured him that he was in good hands, and we quickly went to work. At the hotel coffee shop, I helped him brainstorm a romantic love note, which I wrote up on very nice, expensive stationary and placed in the bedroom of their hotel suite. We decided on a trail of rose petals beginning at the door and ending in a heart shape on the bed for added effect. I also got Mr. Wide Receiver to agree to the idea of placing the ring at the bottom of a champagne glass.

"You can order champagne and chocolate-covered strawberries to be delivered to your room," I suggested. "Then, slip the ring to the waiter—who will get the head's up from me—and he will drop the ring into her glass discreetly before he pours the champagne and leaves the room."

He was very happy with the plans, and when it was all said and done, everything went according to plan—even the part where his girlfriend said "yes".

The following day, however, the athlete came to me and shared a residual concern.

"It's the love note," he confessed. "I think that was what really sealed the deal for her."

"Is that a bad thing?" I wondered.

"Yes! We've created a monster," he joked. "How will I ever recreate that kind of poetry in the future? We set the bar too high!"

Then, turning quite serious, he added: "We're going to have to tell her the truth."

To the NFL superstar's credit, he went ahead that very same day and confessed that the love note was a combined effort, giving me most of the credit. Instead of getting angry, however, the bride-to-be actually laughed heartily at the entire situation. She'd gotten such a kick out of the whole thing but especially out of his acute need to be completely honest for fear she'd see through it all eventually!

"It took a lot of courage for him to ask for help in the first place," she told me later. "He's not one to do that, and I'm honored that he went to so much trouble for me—and then confessed to the truth of it all."

"It sounds to me like a great foundation for a marriage," I said. "Honesty and communication is the key."

I am happy to report that as far as I know, this couple is still very happily married . . . in spite of my heavy-handed helping.

• • •

Back in the late 1980s/early 90s, the Speaker of the House came to our hotel restaurant for lunch. It was a big deal, and the Secret Service was everywhere.

It started as soon as the Speaker's car pulled up to the front of the hotel. A gaggle of burly-looking security guys in mirrored sunglasses jumped out first – to make sure the area was 'secure,' I suppose. Then, while one or two stood watch at the car and another at the entrance to the hotel restaurant, the biggest of all the security guards ushered the Speaker himself from the back of the car into the hotel.

Of course I was intrigued by all the mystique and activity, and I watched as the driver of the car closed the door after the Speaker's exit and walked back around to the driver's side to get back in and await his very important passenger. When he pulled up on his handle, however, he got no response from the door. He pulled again and again and peered into the driver's side and then slammed his fist up against the window. Within seconds, he was running to me for help, completely disheveled.

"I need your security officer to contact the head of the Speaker's detail," he told me. "I've locked myself out of the car, and the keys are still in the ignition."

"We can pop the lock with a coat hanger," I suggested. "We have people lock themselves out of their cars all of the time. Frankie has a great technique perfected."

He looked at me as if I had three heads, and then informed me that this was not exactly a "run-of-the-mill-normal-person" type of car.

"It's as secure as Fort Knox, complete with bullet-proof glass. You can't simply 'pop the lock with a coat hanger'!"

As the luncheon went on I watched, mildly amused, as hordes of Secret Servicemen buzzed through the hotel lobby and outside around it. They reminded me of big black bumblebees in the garden, and I wondered what was going through the minds of our other guests. I imagined some of them speculating that perhaps there'd been a bomb threat or that someone's life was in danger.

It took half an hour for the Secret Service to finally manage to get into the car. For a few weeks after that, the joke around the hotel was, "How many Secret Servicemen does it take to unlock a car door?"

The answer? Five, not including the driver of the car.

•   •   •

It's always fascinating when we have A-list stars staying in our hotels, but most of the time, there is drama to follow. For instance, our hotel was temporarily home to the cast and crew of a big budget film (which meant that there were always paparazzi and fans lurking about hoping to catch a glimpse of the stars). To guard against such media and fan frenzy, hotels have precautions and procedures in place. One of the most common is to book the big leads of a major motion picture in accommodations that are off the Strip, so that these people do not have to walk through a crowded, open lobby.

In this case, the leading man was causing us major headaches because he was never actually spending any time at his off-the-Strip rental. Instead, he strayed everywhere except his comfy, private Vegas digs, making it a nightmare on security all around. On top of it all, his wife called obsessively. At first, we simply said that we couldn't locate him, but soon the word among his crew was that he and his co-star were spending a lot of "off camera" time together.

As it became obvious that the cheating A-lister was never going to be in his villa, it became more difficult for us to cover for him.

We'd gotten the missive from our guest and his handlers to hold all calls from his wife, but this was backfiring at a rapid pace. When we did hold the calls, this only served to infuriate the already-furious wife. She would hang up on us and call her husband's cell phone incessantly. Then, when he wouldn't answer, she'd get back on the phone to us and furiously blast the innocent soul who answered and told her he had no idea where her husband was.

I think eventually the wife got wise to the whole situation and stopped calling the front desk or asking for my services, and while I was thankful for the peace, I couldn't help but feel sorry for her in the midst of the scandal I was sure she would endure.

Sure enough a few months later, the celebrity news magazines had front page stories about Mr. Movie Star's ugly impending divorce. Can we say, "Lights, Camera, Friction?"

• • •

Another case had to do with a legendary rock star. He and his band were staying with us while they played a few dates of their tour in Las Vegas. You can imagine, however, how surprised one of our staff was when he found this popular singer passed out on a landing beside the elevators.

A colleague and I rushed to his side and immediately began performing CPR. When I couldn't detect a pulse, I began to freak out. I didn't wish death on anyone, but I surely didn't want this mega-musician dying on my watch.

Thankfully, the paramedics were quick to arrive and, undaunted, one of them whipped out a huge syringe full of adrenaline. Without warning, one of the EMTs jabbed the needle straight into the rock star's chest. I felt like I was in the middle of a scene from *Pulp Fiction*. This was not the kind of life I was accustomed to living.

Moments later, the formerly comatose rocker sat straight up and mumbled, "What the hell is going on here!?"

The paramedics loaded him onto a stretcher and took him to the hospital for further observation, while everyone at the front desk assumed the big Las Vegas concert that night was off.

A few hours later, our rock star guest strolled back through the lobby as if nothing had happened and headed up to his suite. Apparently, he was not going to let something as trivial as a drug-induced coma get in the way of a good show. Eight hours after lying motionless by a bank of elevators, he was on stage in front of thousands of concertgoers, bellowing out hit songs. File this under sex, drugs and... hard to believe.

Yes, it's always interesting when the big names come for a stay at our hotels, but there is sure to be chaos to follow. So when people say to me that they want to "party like a rock star," I do my best to make magic happen, but I also to avoid the situation of some rock star guests I've witnessed.

• • •

A famous, Italian-born Formula One race car driver was staying at our hotel. Tragically, he was involved in a terrible car accident on the streets of Las Vegas. With severe injuries, he was airlifted to the nearest hospital. One of his legs was badly mangled, but doctors were able to operate right away and save it.

In the meantime, this poor man's wife was back in Europe and only receiving bits and pieces of information. She knew he'd been in a wreck, and she finally found out which hospital her husband was in. However, because she spoke only Italian, when she tried to call the hospital, she was unable to get any information at all. I couldn't imagine how scared she must have been.

Her plight was brought to my attention.

"Wait — I speak a little Italian," I told my boss. "Do you think the hospital would give me her number so that I could help?"

Within a few hours, I was able to start giving her regular updates and kept her informed of everything that the hospital was doing. I even helped her book her trip and arranged to pick her up from the airport myself.

We hit it off famously, and ended up becoming very close during that difficult time. After the operation, the race car driver stayed for a few more weeks at our hotel until he was able to travel. Although the circumstances were very scary and trying, his wife ended up recommending our hotel to many of her well-heeled European friends—which made the hotel managers very happy.

What meant the most to me, however, was the friendship we built and that I was able to help her in what was a very stressful and tragic time. The couple still returns to the hotel often, and I like to think of them as great friends. Strangely enough, even accidents like this have a silver lining.

• • •

I had the pleasure of catering to one of Hollywood's all-time greatest actors, who just so happened to be a beautiful humanitarian and founder of his own food company. This man loved to exercise, but he designed his own clever workout to retain his privacy. Every morning after breakfast, he would use the enclosed hotel stairwells as his exercise room, ascending and descending from floor to floor in the company of a good friend with whom he liked to travel.

The friend alerted me to this habit in advance so that security wouldn't become alarmed at the sight of two older gentlemen going up and down the stairs for an hour or two every day. Armed with this information, I put some notes of encouragement in the stairwell, along with water bottles and towels, all at strategic intervals. He loved it!

For the duration of his stay, he kept telling everyone how delightful he thought the whole thing was. At the end of his stay, he gifted me with a case of very expensive wine as a thank you. He stayed with us again just before his death, and all he could talk about was what might be waiting for him in the stairwell this time! I was saddened at the passing of this lovely star a few years ago, and although I'm sure he'd experienced every level of luxury throughout his years, I was so glad to have interacted with him. I'm happy that my stairwell stunt spoke to him because he's done a lot that has spoken to so many of us.

# Funny in a Peculiar Way

## BUST!

Many times, a concierge will be called into a situation that leaves him/her puzzled and confused. Even those of us who have been around the block a time or two will experience guests or situations that make us wonder about them long after our shift has ended for the day! As you'll see in the following stories, what happens in Vegas . . . is sometimes just weird.

Throughout my career, I have offered management, concierge, and personal assistant services to people in residences and corporate settings, so I've dealt with my fair share of beyond-the-normal-hotel situations. For instance, I once had a gentleman call from a large leased home in a gated Las Vegas community. His issue was that they had no power in the house, and when we arrived, sure enough, not a single indoor light fixture would turn on. In hindsight, I don't know why no one thought to see if the clock on the oven and microwave were working, but instead, a call was put in to the electric company.

Puzzled, the electric company confirmed that the power was up to date; no payments had been missed.

"There should be power flowing to that house right now," my colleague Jim was told.

So Jim did what anyone in his situation would have most likely done; he unscrewed a few light bulbs and examined them. Shaking them gently, he heard the soft tinkle of a burned out lightbulb, and so he moved on to the next one. In short, we realized that every single light bulb in the place was burnt out—and I don't mean twelve or thirteen light bulbs. I mean the lights outside near the garden, the lights by the pool, the overhead lights in every single room – not one light bulb worked!

After going from room to room and checking outside, we finally deduced how every single light bulb in this large home had simultaneously extinguished: the owner of the property was a big NBA star who used the investment residence only sporadically as a starting off point for off-season nightclub expeditions. The athlete and his friends would essentially leave during the night, careful to leave plenty of lights on and timers going. But they were always coming home from their nights of partying in broad daylight, and so they'd never realized that the lights had been left on. The cycle had repeated until evidently, they'd packed up for another basketball season and left without turning off the switches.

Of course, regular people like you and me would have quickly noticed the electricity bill and put an end to it. But the homeowner's business manager had been dutifully paying the electricity bill for months. We ended up itemizing all the different kinds of light bulbs in the house and made a trip to a hardware store to buy sixty-seven light bulbs in all. Just when you think you've seen it all, new light is shed on a unique situation.

• • •

Working in some of the most beautiful hotels in Vegas, I became accustomed to guests being a little bowled over by some of the amenities in their rooms. However, once I had a woman come down to the concierge desk and let me know she had a problem.

"There's a TV set in my room," she said in a thick Eastern European accent with a flustered look on her face.

Puzzled, I waited for her to elaborate. "There's a TV set in my room," she repeated.

I wondered for a moment if she was joking with me, but it was apparent that she was very serious.

"There's a TV in every room," I explained slowly.

"Oh no. I don't want it," she said, shaking her head vigorously.

I assessed her age to be somewhere in her late sixties or early seventies. I wondered if perhaps she was having a problem with the television. Or maybe she didn't understand the way the remote control worked. Then, she added, "I don't want to pay extra."

Then it hit me: she was most likely accustomed to budget travel in Eastern Europe where often there were no televisions in the rooms. Realizing what she thought, I explained that the televisions were amenities, and every guest had one in his or her room.

"So, I can watch for free?" she asked, double-checking with me.

"Absolutely," I assured her. "The only things you have to pay for are premium channels if you order them, like the pay-per-view movies or adult movies. But even then, you'll be asked several times to confirm that you want to order the program."

She took it all in for a moment, looking surprised that she'd be able to watch the TV without paying extra. Then she asked, "What is adult movie?"

I cleared my throat and felt myself blush a little bit. Then I said in a low voice, "It's pornography."

She tilted her head and frowned in confusion. So, I tried again.

"It means sex movies," I said, my cheeks now completely crimson. "Oh!!!" she exclaimed, covering her mouth instantly with her hands, her face now as red as mine. "That's not for me," she said and finally laughed at the situation. She stood there a moment longer and then added, "But I do understand why it cost extra."

•  •  •

Most guests who come to Vegas hotels are a pleasure to serve. The challenge comes, however, while trying to help a guest who is just convinced he/she is right and the concierge is wrong.

This happens quite often when it comes to geography. There were two occasions that really stand out in my memory, and it was interesting to see how the men who thought they were in the know reacted to finding out that they weren't.

Mr. Zhang was visiting us from his home in Hong Kong. He was scheduled to leave Las Vegas for a brief stop home before leaving for an important trip to Calgary. A day or two before he was scheduled to check out of our hotel, he stopped at my concierge desk.

"You have been so helpful always, and I need your help again," he said. "How do I get from Hong Kong to Calgary?"

"Do you want me to get you some flight information?" I asked him as I turned towards my computer.

"No. I'm tired of airplanes. I want to drive."

Puzzled, I sat still for a moment wondering if I'd misunderstood his request. Sensing my confusion, he repeated himself.

"I want to drive to Calgary."

"From Hong Kong?" I questioned.

"Yes," he snapped. I could tell by his tone that he was getting impatient with my stalling.

It was beginning to dawn on me that the man wasn't thinking about the Pacific Ocean he'd have to drive over, but I didn't want to embarrass him. So, I called up a map on my computer and showed him the two locations and the barriers in between.

Seeing this big body of water between his home and his destination seemed to embarrass the guest anyway, and he abruptly stood and walked away. As I watched him stride across the lobby, I wondered if there might not have been a better way to tell him, but I was almost thankful the conversation had ended relatively smoothly.

In other cases, neither party fares as well. I once had three Middle Eastern men come to the desk, and from the very beginning they were rude, aggressive and loud. I try to remember that people of different cultures conduct themselves in different ways, but even so, there are times when I wonder how much rudeness one should allow. Finally, one of the men hushed the others and turned to me to ask me about booking a Grand Canyon tour.

As I was explaining about the West and South Rim, the guest interrupted me and said, "I want to go as close to the mountains as possible."

I nodded. "Right. I understand, sir, but I need a little more information." I explained again about the unique view from the Skywalk if he took the West Rim tour, but that the more famously photographed views—the views he may be more familiar with— were from the South Rim where there were some really nice trails. "Both tours have great things to offer," I said, trying to be helpful.

I was watching the man clenching his jaw and reddening in the face. His breathing was deepening as I was sure he was trying to calm himself as he prayed for patience with me. He interrupted me again. "I don't know what's so hard for you to understand!" he finally shouted.

All heads turned our way, and all eyes were on us—guests, colleagues, anyone in the vicinity.

"I want to get close to the mountains," he said again through his teeth.

I was horrified at this point. It was embarrassing for people to be watching this exchange while I floundered and faltered. I felt that I was doing my best to help this man, but it was obvious he wanted something specific that I wasn't understanding. I didn't know what to say or do. After all, you can only get so close to the "mountains" and I thought I had given him super information with which to make a decision.

Incidentally, I'd never been yelled at by a guest before, and I felt he had crossed a line by basically calling me stupid for the entire hotel lobby to hear. It's safe to say that I was more than a little offended, but after taking a deep cleansing breath, I tried again.

"Sir, I'm sorry. Is there a different way that I could explain it to you? I'm not quite sure what you're asking for."

Well, now the man was absolutely fit to be tied. Leaning forward, while his companions shook their heads and shifted their weight angrily, the man shouted into my face, "Look. I just want to be as close as possible to the faces of your presidents of the United States!"

I have to admit, I felt a little smug when the realization hit me, but I concealed it from my guest, not wanting to give him any ammunition for a second round. Realizing his mistake, however, I no longer felt quite as horrible.

"Sir," I said calmly and with a syrupy sweetness, "You're asking me about tours to the Grand Canyon. The faces of the presidents are not there. They are at Mount Rushmore in South Dakota."

Suddenly, the man froze, realizing that the error had been his, not mine. He actually lowered his eyes and looked sheepishly embarrassed—as well he should have been.

He whirled around on his heel and left my desk as one of his companions coughed out a quiet "thank you" and trailed behind him. Maybe he learned his lesson, though. And maybe next time he'll think about this situation before losing patience with another helpful concierge.

• • •

Our hotel had been open for just a week, so all of the bedding in the rooms was white . . . pristinely white. Since we had some newlyweds checking in, two of us went up to a honeymoon suite to prepare it. We organized the welcome basket and balloon bouquet, checked the mini-bar, and scattered fresh rose petals across the pillows and king-size bed. The effect was beautiful, and I was excited for our newlyweds to see it!

A few hours later, we returned for a final walk-through, and to place champagne and strawberries at their bedside table since the couple was due to arrive in about half an hour. We were absolutely appalled to find that those white sheets were stained red; it looked like a murder scene! We'd had no idea that the fresh rose petals would do that, and just like a couple of criminals trying to cover up a crime, we hurried to clean up the mess.

Stripping the sheets, we frantically called down and had housekeeping bring us fresh ones. We scrambled to pick up all the rose petals, hoping nothing else was stained in the process.

In case you didn't know, making a hotel bed isn't the same as making a bed in the average person's home. There's the mattress protector, the bottom sheet, a top sheet, a blanket, and then the duvet – not to mention the pillowcases – and there's a certain technique and process that makes it all look neat and cozy. It takes time, too, but we were doing our best to rush the process, which meant that we were messing up and having to do bits over to meet hotel standards. By the time we'd finished making the bed as quickly as we could, we were both sweating and breathing heavily.

We were just walking down the hall, rolling our evidence into a housekeeping cart, as a fellow staff member came out of the elevator, escorting the couple to their room. From that point on, I made sure to put all complementary roses in table vases or trail the petals on the floor rather than on white sheets.

• • •

In the not-too-distant past, Las Vegas hotel bellmen took care of guests' luggage in a far more comprehensive manner.

There were these package deals that not only covered airfare and rooms but also included the complementary pick-up and delivery of guests' luggage to and from the airport. Unfortunately, that option was eliminated after 9/11 when travel and airport security measures were tightened.

While the policy was still in place, a woman who had ordered the package and was supposed to be checking out soon called down to the front desk to frantically ask if her luggage had already been sent to the airport. Indeed, it had.

"Oh, dear me! What am I going to do?" she asked.

Before she explained, I had a good idea what had happened.

"Ma'am, would you like me to get you something from one of the hotel boutiques? I'm assuming you're still in your pajamas and forgot to lay out a change of clothes while you were packing your bags."

I heard a soft "ummmm" come through the receiver as she weighed her options. Finally, she thanked me kindly but told me it wouldn't be necessary.

When she came to check out and catch her shuttle to the airport, she was still clad in her pink and purple nightgown with fuzzy slippers. She winked and smiled at me as she waved before stepping into the Las Vegas heat, having decided to make like an eccentric rich person and head to McCarren International Airport in her nightgown.

"I hope she's able to find her suitcase and change before she has to get on the plane," the desk manager said to me, knowing the full story.

I shrugged my shoulders. "Hey, we're in Vegas," I reminded her. "Chances are any onlooker might simply have assumed that the poor lady lost her shirt at the casinos."

But she was not the only one to suffer a wardrobe malfunction.

During this same era and even earlier, gentlemen in Las Vegas were required to wear a dinner jacket, tie, and socks to gain entry into fine dining establishments. No Bermuda shorts or bare-ankle loafers were allowed. A particular guest staying with us during this bygone era had packed his dress shoes but forgotten to bring socks.

He came to my desk to see what he could do, but it was late, and there were no shops open where he could purchase what he needed.

"I'm so sorry," I said. "I'm not sure what else I could suggest since everything is closed for the evening and your reservations are quite soon."

I saw him eyeing the desk manager, and I thought for a second he might ask him to borrow his socks, so I inserted a joke to steer him away from the awkwardness.

"You know, if you brought shoe polish, you could always just coat your ankles with that."

He didn't laugh or say anything in response, so I figured he just didn't think my joke was that funny. The very next afternoon, however, he appeared at my desk again.

"Thanks for the tip," he said, but I had to wrack my brain to remember what tip I'd given him. "The shoe polish?" he provided.

I felt my stomach plunge. Surely he hadn't?

"Only problem is, I'm not sure how to get it off, and my wife won't let me join her at the pool until I get it cleaned up."

Of course, I immediately looked down at the man's ankles to see a thick, rough circle about two inches in thickness encircling his ankles.

I couldn't believe it! The man had obviously failed to realize that I had been joking and for some reason, his wife hadn't deterred him from this hare-brained idea.

From that point on, I was very careful to make sure my guests knew when I was joking!

• • •

When I first started to work as a concierge, I came across a mango sitting on the ground in front of my desk. I went to my manager and said, "Look what I found."

"Oh, a mango," was her response, and that was all.

I chuckled a bit and asked, "Is it yours?"

When she told me that it wasn't, I threw it in the trash.

A little while later, my manager asked me what I did with the mango.

"I threw it away," I said.

Shaking her head, she informed me of my policy violation. "No. You have to turn it into the Lost and Found department."

I stood there for a moment, waiting for her to laugh, but it became apparent that she wasn't joking.

"Are you serious?" I asked.

"Very serious," she replied. "Once, we had a security officer who picked up a penny and put it into his pocket. Because he didn't turn it in, and it happened to be some guest's lucky penny, he got suspended."

I was torn; a part of me was shocked at this story. It seemed so harsh and cruel, which made the other part of me suspect that my manager was playing a joke on me; after all, I was a rookie.

Still, I didn't want to end up losing my job over a mango, and I was okay with being the butt of a joke if it came down to it, so I called security.

"I found a mango. Should I turn it in to you guys?"

There was a pause on the line before the man on duty asked me if I was crazy. I laughed, hung up, and forgot about it.

The very next day, my manager approached me.

"What did you do with the mango? Did you turn it in to security?" she asked.

"No," I told her. "I called, and they asked me if I was crazy."

"Well, we just had a guest come by looking for a mango," she said.

Already I was seeing how this would play out, and I smirked a little at my boss to let her know I was onto her.

"Where was the mango from?" she asked.

I shook my head and replied, "There was a Venezuela sticker on it."

"Oh, that's a relief," she said, her face brightening. "Couldn't have been the same mango. Our customer was looking for a mango that was grown in the US."

To this day, I have no idea whether my manager was pulling my leg, but whether she was or not, the incident did the trick; I always make sure I turn everything in to Lost and Found!

•    •    •

An older woman was checking in, and it was clear from the moment I laid eyes on her that she wasn't a happy camper. Her face was drawn into a deep frown, and her eyes seemed to pull downward. I could almost see the steam coming from her ears, and she was still flushed from the anger I could feel coming from her. She proceeded to let me know that her flight had been delayed, her luggage was temporarily lost, and her taxi cab driver had decided to take the "scenic route" just so he could charge her more. The way she told me all of this, however, gave me the distinct impression that the woman felt as if this was all my fault—her finger jabbing the air in front of me and her eyes narrowing at me as she spoke.

I asked her politely what had brought her to Las Vegas.

"I'm playing in the poker tournament," she barked at me.

"Cool!" I said. "Maybe all of that needed to happen so that you get your bad luck behind you."

She began retelling me all of the bad luck she'd just experienced, and where I could, I offered what help I could. For the ones I couldn't do anything about (the driver of the cab, the flight delay), I just listened and expressed my own chagrin as she gave me details. Little by little, this angry tiger turned into a purring kitten as she got all of those irritations off her chest. We got her checked into her room, and I personally escorted her to the lounge where the poker tournament would take place.

As I was turning to go, the woman – who was old enough to be my grandma – put her hand on my arm and said, "Oh come on. You're not going to stay and have a drink?"

Of course, I couldn't because I was on duty. Instead, I patted her hand amiably and said, "I can't right now, but after your day, you deserve to drink one for you and me both!"

She laughed, winked at me, and told me she'd do just that. When she waltzed into the lounge, I saw her wave at a few people and smile. I was so glad that I'd been able to turn her frown—and hopefully her bad luck—upside down.

• • •

When I first began working as a concierge, I helped a lot of big Italian high-rollers. There were all sorts of transportation requests to process. One night, I looked up from my desk to see twenty Italian men approaching the desk. They wanted to book flights back home to Italy; all twenty at one time, and they wanted to be on the same flight. With the online system, I could only book ten flights at a time, so I booked those ten with the intention of booking the other ten immediately.

Unfortunately, when I pressed the back button, the time and date switched, but I hadn't realized it. I had ten of my Italians booked on a flight the next day, while the other ten were booked for some time in the future. Of course, when they went to the airport, ten had the flight while the other ten didn't. I was off for the next two days, and rather than going to the concierge on duty, they waited for me to come back to work. That gave them plenty of time for their anger and frustration to grow to epic proportions, and I later wondered how many different ways they'd discussed murdering me by the time I got back to work.

I'd hardly been at the desk twenty minutes before the ten of them approached and showed me the receipt for the flight tickets. That's when I noticed it had the wrong date.

I panicked! These were very important guests, and I had messed their flights up. I called the airline only to be told that they could have reimbursed the guests within twenty-four hours of booking. Instead, it had been more than two days! Refusing to refund the money, the airline gave the men a credit for the following year.

The leader of the group completely lost it. He was saying all sorts of things that his friend was happy to translate for me. There were numerous expletives, and he threatened that he'd never use my concierge service again.

All of this was completely out of my control. Sometimes you win, sometimes you lose, and sometimes you just "plane" mess up!

# Crimes and Misdemeanors

## Counting Their Cards

Occasionally, a concierge is asked to do something illegal or unethical. Of course, he or she will not do anything illegal for a guest, but letting the guest know that can sometimes be difficult. In fact, these situations can often be extremely uncomfortable, and even funny at times. As you'll see from the following stories, guests often think that a concierge can literally get them anything they want!

"Hey there," a hotel guest approached me one sunny afternoon. "What can you tell me about the best night clubs around here?"

We chatted for a little while as I regaled him with details about some of the hot spots. I told him about some of my favorite DJs in the area and about different types of clubs. Before he left, he wrote something on a piece of paper and slid it over to me.

"I need a favor," he said, his hand still on the paper. "My friends and I want to party at a few clubs tonight. On that paper is the combination to my hotel room safe. Here's three hundred dollars."

I looked at him a bit confused. He winked. "We want to party at all the best places all night long," he informed me. "Just see what you can do for three hundred."

It dawned on me what he was requesting: obviously, he wanted a car service to take him and his friends to and from the clubs and bring them back safely at the end of the night. I could set up the itinerary and driver, and I was pretty sure that I could get him a decent experience for three hundred bucks.

"No problem," I said to my guest.

"Really? You're awesome!" He smiled a toothy grin and said, "Don't lose that combination."

I held up the paper. "Got it!"

It wasn't until he had gone that I thought it was a bit odd that this operation had to be so covert, but perhaps he wanted to take the credit for lining up a memorable evening for his friends, or maybe he thought I would need more than three hundred dollars.

The detail kept nagging at me. Puzzled, I told my colleague about it.

As I was relaying the story, a knowing look spread over his face, and he nodded with a low laugh.

"Do you know what he wants from you?" he asked me.

"I think he wants me to set it all up, get him a driver, and give him an itinerary for the evening," I replied.

A short burst of laughter escaped from my colleague's mouth. "Not even close," he replied. "He wants you to score him some dope."

My own mouth dropped open, and I felt my heart begin to race with this knowledge.

"You know what I mean? He wants you to get him some drugs."

"I know what you mean," I finally answered, "I just can't believe that's what I agreed to do."

"The money is to pay for them, and he wants you to put them in his hotel room safe."

"How could I have possibly misunderstood that?" I asked myself and my colleague.

He answered with a laugh and a pat on the back. "Not everyone is as pure as the driven snow as you are, obviously."

I gripped his arm quickly. I was beginning to realize the trouble I'd gotten myself into. "Oh my gosh," I said to my colleague. "I had no idea." Of course, there was no way I would be going out onto the Strip to try and score some recreational drugs, but I dreaded the conversation with the man. I had to track down the guest and give back his money.

"I'm sorry, sir," I said. "I misunderstood you. I can make arrangements for your night, but I can't help you with your other request."

The guest wasn't fazed as he accepted the money back. He shrugged. "That's okay," he said. "I actually just scored," he gestured to his phone, "so I'm all set. Thanks for everything, though."

I made my escape quickly before he revealed anything else I really didn't want to know.

• • •

A happy guest in a Hawaiian-printed shirt came up to the concierge desk one day.

"Good afternoon," I greeted. "Can I help you with something?"

He wouldn't quite meet my eyes, seeming shy and awkward. He shifted his weight from one foot to the other a few times, before he finally said, "I have a question for you. It's going to be kind of weird."

"I'm pretty accustomed to 'weird,'" I told him. "After all, we are in Las Vegas."

He leaned closer to my desk and said very low, "I need some marijuana."

"Oh," I said. "Well, that's not the weirdest request I've had, I'll have to tell you. And I can often accommodate weird, but that is something that is strictly prohibited."

The man put his hands up and shook his head. "It's not what you think. I actually have a prescription for medical marijuana. I have glaucoma."

I didn't know what this guy was getting at. If that were the case, why was he asking the concierge about this? I pretended to think through his latest information. "I apologize," I said, finally, "but I don't think there's any place in Las Vegas that would fill a prescription for medical marijuana."

The man frowned and said, "Is there nothing you can think of?"

"There's a Walgreens just up the street. I can give you directions," I smiled. "That's the only thing I can suggest, though."

I watched his eyes narrow as he worked his jaw back and forth. He was seeing that he wasn't going to get anywhere with me.

"Well, thanks for nothing," he said. "Guess I'll just have to work this one out myself." He turned on his heel and was gone before I could utter another word.

Several hours later, I spotted the same guest enjoying himself by the pool with a couple of friends, and I wondered if he'd found a pharmacist or not. Judging by the amount of room service he ordered later, I'd be willing to bet that he had.

• • •

One of our guests was turning twenty-one and would be celebrating in Las Vegas. Prior to her arrival, the girl's wealthy mother called me to make special arrangements.

"I have some gifts I'd like her to have while she's there," the mother explained to me on the phone. "Can I simply send them to you via Fed-Ex, and you'll make sure they get to her room before she checks in?"

"Certainly," I assured the mom. I thought it was so sweet for the mother to make sure her daughter had presents from her to open even on her twenty-first birthday.

"I'll send the items in one shipment, but can you gift-wrap them for me?" the mother asked.

Of course, I told her that I'd be happy to oblige.

When the shipment arrived, I gathered up tissue paper and gift bags, ribbons, and boxes. Imagine my surprise when I opened the box to find that it was filled with a variety of sexy lingerie and sex toys, from fur-lined handcuffs and nipple clamps to vibrators and flavored oils and lotions.

I quickly slammed the box shut, my face almost as red as if my own mother had sent me the box. I had to gather my wits and complete the wrapping I had promised.

Mom and daughter were both from Los Angeles, a town where it is not unusual for rich parents to give young daughters the gift of breast augmentation surgery or Botox treatments as coming-of-age gifts. Still, it felt decidedly odd to be lining up the daughter for a debauched birthday celebration. It was an upbringing quite opposite to my own, but who was I to judge? Perhaps I'd lived too sheltered a life.

I wondered again at the protected bubble I seemed to have been raised in when the daughter approached my desk shortly after checking in.

"Do you know Tina?" she asked. "Is Tina in town?"

I stood there a moment and thought, *Tina Turner hasn't been to Vegas in some time.* The only other celebrity with the name "Tina" that I could think of was Tina Fey, and I'd heard nothing about her being in the area.

I looked at the daughter, who had cocked her head as she waited patiently for my response.

*Come on*, I said to myself. *Tina... Tina. You've got to know who this is.*

Finally, I shrugged. "Sorry," I said, "I don't know who Tina is."

She mirrored my shrug and smiled as she said in a rather chipper voice, "Never mind. It's okay," before she headed out to the pool.

I knew this was a big birthday, and I wanted her stay to be as memorable as possible, so I decided to ask a co-worker if he could help me out.

As soon as I relayed the guest's question to him, he held up his hand and stopped me. "'Tina' means drugs. She was asking you to help her get some drugs, or give her information about where to get them here."

I was floored, and I tried to wrap my brain around how the name "Tina" had anything to do with procuring drugs at all. It seemed this guest (and her mother) were determined to educate me about these worlds that I had no clue even existed.

From all that my guest told me upon checking out, she had the most wonderful birthday stay. Judging by the variety of young men I saw her with during her stay, her mom's gifts were well used. As for Tina? The only Tina I knew kept singing her most famous chorus in my head each time I saw the daughter with another man on her arm: "What's love got to do, got to do with it?"

• • •

One particular afternoon, a middle-aged Kentucky man asked for my help in purchasing a gift for his girlfriend.

"I want to buy her something feminine and pretty," he said. "Maybe some lingerie or pajamas."

I nodded and said, "That's a great idea. There are a number of fabulous shops nearby where you could find the perfect gift."

The man nodded and said, "Well, what kind of lingerie do *you* think is the best?"

I thought for a moment. "I think it's important to find something that reminds you of your girlfriend. I'd suggest going into a shop and looking at some of their lingerie on display. Something will probably strike you as an outfit she would like or one that you would like to see her in. That's how I would approach it if it were me."

He nodded and thanked me and headed out, I assumed, to an adult shop down the Strip. Later on that evening, I overheard one of the maids complaining to her supervisor.

"And then he asked me what kind of lingerie I liked best," she was saying.

A mental red flag went off, and I inserted myself into the conversation.

"Sorry to eavesdrop," I interrupted. "But did a guest ask you that question?"

The maid nodded. "He came in while I was finishing his room. We got to talking, and he told me he wanted to buy lingerie for his girlfriend. Then he started asking me all these questions."

"A nice-looking Southern gentleman?"

Again she nodded.

"He came to my desk asking the same sort of thing. I hope he didn't make you too uncomfortable."

The maid, known to be a bit of a spitfire, shook her head. "Before he could ask me too much more, I told him that my boyfriend bought most of my lingerie, and that he was a professional wrestler and bodyguard. That seemed to shut the guest up pretty quickly."

I laughed, but little did I know that I would have another encounter with the guest the next day.

"Thanks for your help yesterday," he smiled, "but I think I just got myself more confused than anything. So much to choose from."

"I'm sorry about that," I said, hoping that I could look busy and give him the hint that I couldn't talk. He didn't take the hint, though.

Instead, he said, "So, I guess I'll have to rely on your help some more. Like, tell me what style of bra do you think is sexiest?"

At this point, I started to feel uncomfortable. This man was way more focused on my own likes and dislikes than he was on his supposed girlfriend's. I tried to remain professional yet aloof when I replied, "I don't know. You should probably think about what she usually wears."

After a moment, the man asked, "What is your size? I think she's close to the same size. Oh, and have you ever worn crotchless panties? I'm thinking that's something she might think was sexy, but . . . I don't know. What do you think?"

Beyond creeped out by the conversation, I decided it was high time to cut him off. I curtly told the man that I couldn't help him and walked back to my manager's office where I could hide from the guest.

"What are you doing?" the manager asked me.

I told him the entire story, including the exchange with the maid, and I watched as my manager became more and more agitated. Apparently, a female guest had complained of a male guest asking inappropriate questions about her choice in lingerie and bust size, etc. while they were at the pool. My manager was not happy that this so-called gentleman had accosted two employees and one guest ... that we knew of so far.

A few weeks later, I heard through the hotel grapevine that a gentleman had been busted by police at another property on the Strip after actually trying to steal women's underwear from a room. The perpetrator turned out to be – that's right – Mr. Kentucky. Don't say women's intuition isn't right on the money.

# Heartfelt Moments

## Winning the Pot

Sometimes, concierges are blessed enough to build wonderful relationships with the families and individuals they serve. Other times, they're trusted enough to be allowed to share in some wonderful moments. As with any other job dealing with people, building bonds and attachments is easy. As you can imagine, these concierges might be subjected to a whole range of different emotions ... and most of them wouldn't change it for the world!

There have been many funny moments in my concierge career, but the most meaningful moments have allowed me to form close relationships with some of my regular guests. One such example is the Braxton family from Mobile, Alabama. They are one family that means a lot to me. They began coming to our hotel in the mid-1990s, when their daughter was just nine years old. She was quite a character, always wanting to do the craziest things and try whatever looked fun. I remember her dancing in the lobby as the pianist played, unashamed and unembarrassed as she twirled around perfect strangers. She would be mesmerized by the lights of the casino, and she even told me once she was "going gambling" when I asked her where she was off to one evening.

The family returned every year, which afforded me the opportunity to really get to know them and become close friends. They always asked for me specifically whenever they were visiting.

Tragically, at the age of seventeen, the daughter was diagnosed with cancer. I remember the shock that I felt when I found out, and I could only imagine how it had thrown her parents into a tragic tailspin of emotions, leaving them feeling sucker-punched in the gut. The family decided that rather than cancelling their annual trip, they would still come to Vegas, as long as Lucy was able to travel. After all, it was her favorite place in the world.

Though they came, she was unable to attend some of the planned outings at the last minute due to the effects of chemotherapy. It broke my heart to see her weakened and frail, sometimes to the point of being confined to a wheelchair. I hated that she had to be excluded, and whenever I could, I would do my best to provide some diversion for her at the hotel. It was hard to see her suffer, this girl who had been so completely filled with life prior to her illness. Through it all, I was constantly amazed by her strength and her courage.

A few years later, on their annual trip, she waltzed up to me, threw her arm around my shoulders, pulled me in close to her, and announced that she was cancer-free! We whooped and hollered, overjoyed at the fact that she had finally beaten her cancer into remission. She introduced me to her closest friend, whom she had brought along to celebrate with her.

"But it's a double celebration," Lucy informed me. "I'm turning twenty-one on the trip too!" And she winked at me as if we had already concocted some secret plan.

I could tell her spunk had returned ten-fold.

"Dad says that Shelly and I can go out to a nightclub on our own for my birthday," she beamed. But when she told me which nightclub she was hoping to frequent—one of the saucier nightclubs on the Strip—I immediately wondered how dear old Dad would feel about that.

"That's why you're going to have to arrange it for me," she whispered, "and I'll take care of things with my parents. I won't lie," she answered before I asked. "We'll go to the nightclub I tell them we're going to, but then you'll send us a car to take us to the other one later on."

I looked over my imaginary spectacles at her, my mouth twisting to one side in contemplation.

"Don't worry," she said. "We'll be fine. And I know you'll make sure we get home safe and sound, too."

I didn't feel good about going behind her parents' backs. I respected them too much and valued their friendship and trust, but I didn't want to let Lucy down or breach the trust she'd placed in me. I felt myself between a rock and a hard spot there. If anything were to go wrong, it would be my responsibility, and I'd never be able to live with myself or face her parents if anything happened.

This is just proof: as a concierge, there are situations that need to be nimbly handled. So, without telling the daughter or her friend, I discreetly let the parents in on the little secret, got their okay, and got them to stay quiet about it.

When it was all said and done, and the night of partying was over, the girls were returned to the hotel safe and sound—just as Lucy had predicted—and the parents were in the know the entire time, lessening any worries that may have been and soothing my own troubled soul in the process.

I'd proven to them how trustworthy I was, and the next year, they let the girls come to Vegas on their own—as long as I was working, and they could count on me to help them out. I really love being a friend of the family.

•   •   •

When I plan a day out or make arrangements for a show, it's always important to me that my guests have a wonderful time. I'm sure they always anticipate a great time as well, but to most of us, a day out is just another link in a long chain of memories. On one particular occasion, I was asked to plan an outing that was so much more than that. A colleague of mine was staying at the hotel with a very good friend of his.

This friend, Cynthia, had been diagnosed with terminal brain cancer, and my colleague Stan wanted to give her the best weekend possible, to make wishes come true. He wanted to make it very special, and he confided in me that this would likely be the last trip Cynthia would take in her life. She was scheduled for some very aggressive chemotherapy that her doctors didn't expect to make much of a difference. They only expected her to have a few more months of precious life.

As you might imagine, when I learned this, it suddenly turned into the most important moment of my career. Here I was, asked to plan what was probably going to be the last joyous occasion this young woman would remember. I found out that she had a very soft spot toward animals, and I had some contacts with the local zoo. I knew that some baby orangutans had just been born about a month prior, so I called the director of services and explained the whole situation. His immediate willingness to help was so touching that I got tears in my eyes.

"I'll give them the royal treatment," he promised. "I'll meet them at the gate and give them a private tour of the entire operation. Then, I'll make certain Cynthia gets some one-on-one time with the new babies."

I could not have asked for more, and I was moved again at how accommodating the zoo staff was being for someone they'd never even met.

On the scheduled day, one of our hotel cars drove Stan and Cynthia to the zoo, where they spent the entire day. The director's promises were all met, and Stan and Cynthia were able to take in every animal show while they were there, sometimes even being invited onstage to help with the animals.

When they returned, Cynthia was beaming, her smile reaching from ear to ear. I was certain I was seeing pure joy on her face. She came right up to me, gave me a huge hug and kiss, and said, "You won't believe all we saw!"

For the next few minutes, she gushed about the fun they'd had, and how they'd held and played with the baby orangutans.

"They even played ball with me," she said excitedly. She showed me pictures on her phone of her and the animals. When she looked up with glistening eyes at me, I knew I would have to struggle to hold back the tears myself.

"I can't explain to you what this means to me."

Now, my colleague had not told her that I knew about her condition because she didn't want anyone to know. But it was all I could do to fight to keep my own tears from flowing.

I swallowed hard and smiled my biggest, most hospitable smile, and said, "I'm so happy! We just wanted to make sure you had a great time and could tell your friends how nice your stay was."

As the doctors predicted, Cynthia passed away a few months after that, but I'll never forget the look on her face when she returned from the zoo. It still means the world to me that I was able to play a small role in helping to give her that beautiful memory before she passed.

And I'm grateful for the memory, too.

• • •

I've handled a lot of wedding arrangements for guests, and I've both lived through and heard a lot of very touching wedding stories from my fellow concierges – but the one that is most moving for me happened over a July 4th weekend in Vegas.

"My daughter and her fiancé are both in the service," a lady said to me on the telephone one May, "and they are both currently serving in Iraq. They are in two separate parts of the country, and while my daughter is relatively safe where she is stationed, her fiancé is on the front lines."

I expressed my sympathy and asked how I could help.

"They are going to be on leave this summer," she said, "and they want to be married in Las Vegas, in your hotel.

"Exciting!" I said with sincerity, for I have a soft spot for those who serve our country, and I love a good wedding.

"They need to buy rings and flowers, rent tuxes, *everything*," the mother informed me, "because they won't have anything with them. Also, it is important to them that they do not get married in a chapel. Is that something you can arrange?"

"I have lots of resources," I said, "so we'll make their wishes come true for sure."

I was excited about helping this soldier-couple. Briefly, before I'd become a concierge, I'd worked as a flight attendant with a small charter airline. We transported American troops to and from the war in Iraq. It might not have been a very important job to some people, but I took it very seriously. It allowed me to do some small part to take care of our soldiers – the men and women who fought for us daily. So, when I heard this story, it instantly became very close to my heart, and it was important for me to help.

The mother and I were on the phone constantly over the next two months, trying to pin down an exact date, but it was very difficult because no one knew precisely when the leave was going to happen, and when the couple would arrive. In addition to this, the couple was a young military couple; they didn't have a lot of money to spend on the wedding. So, while we waited to confirm the exact date, I went ahead making plans.

The first bit of luck came to me from our hotel. There was a fabulous area on the thirty-second floor that was a seating area; it had a gorgeous view of the Strip and was absolutely perfect for a small wedding of ten to fifteen people. When I found out I could reserve it for free, I was thrilled! As I made the plans, everyone else's patriotic spirits soared – they'd hear about the couple and want to do something for them. Our hotel bakery agreed to make the couple a beautiful cake at no cost. I found an officiator who wanted to marry the couple on his own time without charging them a dime, and I was even able to get a few restaurants to agree to feed the guests and wedding party for just $25 a plate – a fabulous price for these outstanding Vegas restaurants.

We finally had everything ready – and shortly after all our plans were laid, we found out when the couple would arrive. The family and friends met the couple at the airport, where the daughter arrived bawling her eyes out. Her fiancé, who was an intimidatingly tough, muscular private, also couldn't keep the tears from falling. It was an extremely touching moment. When they got to the hotel, I sent the couple straight to their room where champagne and solitude awaited them, knowing they'd just spent thirty-five hours on a plane trying to get back to one another.

The wedding the next day was gorgeous, and everything went off without a hitch. The hardest part was keeping the bride from ruining her make-up with all the tears that spilled down her cheeks. The couple was incredibly touched by everything I'd done to make their stay so special. However, the light mood was darkened when they received a message that their leave had been cut short, and they had to depart the next day.

If I could have screamed, I would have. In my mind, however, I was yelling, *No! You've got to be joking! This poor couple.*

I'll admit, concierges can do a lot of things, but directing the military is a bit beyond our control. Still, I felt like I had to do something.

I picked up the phone and called Fort Bragg in North Carolina, thinking that I could explain the situation to someone. I did – several times and to several different people. I kept getting directed here and there, and spoke to so many people I was losing track of them, and slowly, I felt myself losing hope.

Finally, I spoke to a two-star general. I sighed as I introduced myself and told the story for what had to be the twentieth time. Then he interrupted me, asking for my name again.

"Weren't you a flight attendant?" he asked suddenly, and the flame of hope flickered a little brighter within me.

"Yes," I said.

"Got long blonde hair and blue eyes?" he asked.

"I do."

"You attended my last flight home from Iraq," he informed me.

You could have knocked me down with a feather. "I'm so glad you remember me, sir! I hope that means I made a good impression," I said smiling, hope raging like wildfire now.

"Tell me the story again," he said, and this time he listened carefully until the very end without interrupting.

"Let me see what I can do," he said. "I'll never forget the special care you took of me and my buddies on that flight. You couldn't tell us enough times how heroic we were. I'd love to help return a favor for you and these two love-birds."

He called me back within a few hours. Not only was he able to get this couple's leave extended for three more days, but he paid for their room during the extension! I was ecstatic for them, and when they received the news, they rushed to my desk to thank me.

"We can't believe it!" the woman said. "We'll never be able to repay you."

I smiled and winked. "I know a two-star general who told me he'd never be able to repay my kindness, yet life granted him the opportunity to do just that! You just never know the opportunities life will present us with. Besides, this is just something small I can do for you . . . after everything you do for us and this country. . . consider it a feeble way for me to repay you."

They do repay me, though. Every year I get their Christmas card and some wonderful gift. It's more than enough just to be a part of their lives and their story.

• • •

One of my most memorable guests was a young man called Vince who was dying of cancer. He called me up one day and asked me to help him plan out his Vegas vacation with his family.

"This is most likely to be the last vacation I will ever experience," he told me. "I want it to be the most amazing time they could ever imagine. When I'm gone, I want them to have these great memories of our perfect Vegas vacation."

I was already choking back the tears, but he continued to give me more information and provided me with a list of requests.

"Let's just please make it incredible for them," he said. "It's going to be my way of saying 'thank you' and 'goodbye' to the people who have supported me my entire life."

Wiping a tear from my cheek, I said into the phone, "Vince, I'm simply honored to be a part of such a significant time for you—and your family. I'm touched that you would share so much of your story with me. You could have easily regaled me with a list of needs and requests without giving me the details, but you were very candid, and I thank you so much for honoring me enough to do that."

"It's vital that you know how important this vacation is to me," he said. "I also didn't want anyone to say anything to you and catch you off-guard. If you see my mom crying, you'll know it wasn't because someone was mean to her; she's just been very emotional with the whole thing."

I was amazed at how he was able to simply talk about his impending death as if it were any other event in his life, and I admired that he was living by this philosophy.

I learned through a few of our conversations that he adored golf, and so as a special surprise to him, I made arrangements for him and his dad to play on one of the best courses in Vegas. I planned outings and activities that he could do with his family, so that they could spend every available minute together. They got the best seats at the top shows and had prime reservations at the best restaurants. Everything fell into place to bring them all the best vacation they'd ever had, despite the bitter-sweetness of the situation.

For a long time after the family had gone, I found myself thinking of them and wondering how they were and what had become of them. I wondered how they were each handling the passing, if it had occurred already. I thought of Vince, how young he'd been and how sweet and appreciative he had been to everyone he had come in contact with. About a year after their visit, I got a phone call. I answered the phone, and the man's voice on the other end sounded oddly familiar.

"Mary?" the voice asked.

"This is Mary," I answered.

"Weren't you the concierge about a year ago?" came the voice.

"Yes. I've been at this hotel for about six years now," I explained. "Is this a former guest?"

"It is," the voice said enigmatically. "I came and brought my family about a year ago for the vacation of a lifetime. You helped me schedule everything for the most important family vacation of my life."

I felt goosebumps break out all over my skin as the voice began to plant a seed of recognition in my brain.

"Now, I'm going to need your help to plan the second vacation of a lifetime," the voice said.

"Vince?" I whispered almost inaudibly, for I was half-believing the call had come from the other side.

Suddenly, he exclaimed, "I lived, Mary! I lived!"

I couldn't help myself; I was so happy that it was difficult for me to even speak, but thankfully, Vince took on the responsibility, telling me all that he'd like to do on his next family trip to Vegas.

He has returned to the hotel many times since then and has become a part of many different charities, being quite the activist for cancer research. He has given more of himself than he ever thought possible to give and spends a lot of time working with kids who have been diagnosed with cancer. I know without a doubt that this young man was able to live for a reason. It just goes to show you that even when you think it's the end, often the best is yet to come.

•  •  •

Once, I had a large group of Russian tourists booked into a block of suites in the hotel. After a fun-filled stay, they decided they'd bonded so much, they all wanted to go home on the same flight. The group came to me to help them change the times of their departures and get tickets to ensure that everyone could go home on the same plane.

Everyone, that is, except for one.

Yes, in all of the hubbub and chaos of trying to get everyone booked, somehow one person had slipped through the cracks and knew nothing of the plans. Apparently, Nika was enjoying some time at the spa when the rest of her party checked out and somehow failed to realize that she was missing. (It sounds impossible, but I'll remind you of the movie *Home Alone,* and you'll remember how easily done it actually is.)

When Nika went back to her room, she was locked out. She came to my desk dressed in a robe from the spa, speaking frantically in Russian and crying. While I couldn't understand what she was saying, those tears were a language we all understand.

I could tell that she was confused and terrified. Who wouldn't be? By the time we were finally able to put the pieces of the puzzle together enough to understand each other, her group had boarded their plane and was on their way back to the Motherland.

She didn't speak a word of English, but we were able to at least locate her suitcase, which had been turned in by the maids cleaning the room. I was so upset for her that I even ended up calling my own husband.

"Can you imagine?" I asked him. "If that had been me at a young age – a girl left behind in another country – I would have been terrified!"

"Doesn't anyone there speak any Russian?" he asked, and I hung up the phone and embarked on my new quest. I needed to find someone to talk to this girl, but I also needed to figure out a place to put her. I had another huge group checking in within hours, and therefore didn't have a vacant room in the entire hotel.

Finally, I found a girl in housekeeping who spoke Russian, and through her, I explained to Nika that she would be coming home with me until new travel arrangements were made.

Even though the Russian teenager and I spoke two different languages, we got along famously. I made her dinner, and took her for a walk around the neighborhood. We laughed as we both tried to explain things to each other by pointing and gesturing. I tried to point out objects and tell her what they were in English. She would nod, comprehending, and then tell me the name of it in Russian. We had a lot of fun, and I was surprised to find that despite the language barrier, I was making a new friend.

Though my guest was only supposed to stay with me that first night, it ultimately took three days for us to book her on a new flight to Russia. We said goodbye at the airport. I knew she was thankful for what I had done for her, but I, too, was thankful for a new friendship and a renewed belief in the inherent goodness of people.

After this unexpected little adventure, my husband started to tease me at dinner every night, asking, "So, who are you bringing home tomorrow? Maybe a Chinese man or a lady from France? Let's hope for the latter—France and America need to improve their relations, and I have confidence that it could start with you."

I still get Christmas cards from my Russian friend, even though it's been many years now since her extended stay. The trip to Vegas was the only time she ever traveled to the U.S. and each year, she signs her holiday card with the same funny greeting – "Wishing I were (still) there."

• • •

Unfortunately, accidents do happen while guests are staying in Vegas, and sometimes, those accidents are very serious. There have been a few times when I've had to comfort guests and help make arrangements that were not celebratory or happy at all.

There was a Japanese couple who was visiting us for the first time. At first, I barely remembered them until I got a call from Hawaii one day.

"I'm very concerned about my friend," the man on the phone said. "I know he and his wife are staying with you, but I've called their room several times for two and a half days now and can't get any answer. I leave messages, but they haven't returned my calls."

"Would you like us to check on them?" I offered.

"Please," he replied. "I know they don't speak much English at all. They are from Japan. I just want to know that they are okay. Do you think that you can somehow have them call me?"

I smiled. "Believe it or not, I speak Japanese," I told him, and he was very relieved when I said that I would go and check on them myself and assist them in calling him.

When I got to their room, sure enough, they were there, and the message light on their phone was blinking non-stop. I asked them in Japanese if everything was okay. I could see the relief on their faces when they heard their native language, and the first thing they asked was how to get the red light to stop its infernal blinking.

Once I'd assisted them, and they'd heard the messages from their friend, I helped them make the phone call to him. When I left their room, I could hear them laughing and explaining about the nice Japanese-speaking lady. They had not thought anyone would be able to help them at all and were too afraid to ask.

A few hours later, the man came down to my desk and pushed a crisp twenty-dollar bill across to me. He told me he was so thankful for my help, and I knew exactly how much this meant, coming from a man whose country did not practice gratuities for services.

The next day, however, tragedy struck. The phone rang, and when I picked it up, all I could hear was a string of wails in Japanese. I finally got it out of the wife that something was wrong with her husband, so I sent our first responders and called 911.

It was too late. Her husband had had a heart attack and died.

Feeling a connection with the couple and not wanting her to be alone, I accompanied the wife to the hospital and served as translator for her. I did all I could to comfort her throughout the ordeal, but I couldn't imagine how sad and scared she must have been.

She hasn't been back to Vegas – and who can blame her – but every now and then, I receive a letter from my new friend. From tragedy sometimes friendship blooms, and I'm just glad I could be there when she needed me most.

• • •

Another time, one of my guests passed away during his stay. He was an older gentleman, and I recalled helping him just the day before he passed. He was quite elderly and so brittle that he could barely stand. Wisely, he'd rented an electric scooter to help him get around town. The day before, he had pulled up to my desk, risen from his scooter, and pulled a crinkled piece of paper from his pocket.

He had put the paper on my desk and slowly and carefully smoothed it out. It became immediately clear that his vision had also weakened with age, as he'd pulled out a flashlight and a magnifying glass. With one hand he held the flashlight, and with the other the magnifying glass, then he stooped over the paper and started to read its contents aloud to me.

"Oh, it's your boarding pass information for tomorrow," I said with realization.

"Can you check me in from here?" he asked me.

"We can take care of that in the morning if you like," I told him. We had a line, naturally, and everyone was standing on tip-toe, leaning in close to see what this colorful, endearing gentleman was doing. I couldn't help but smile in admiration, hoping that when I was his age, I'd feel spry enough to take trips on my own like that.

We set it up for him to come and check in at a certain time, and he wrote the information down in a little notebook. I could tell that he took great pride in the fact that he could still handle his business, and he was so charming and endearing that not a single person in the line complained or even sighed as he carefully relayed the information, refolded the paper, gathered his tools, and returned everything to his fanny pack.

When he didn't arrive the next morning at the appointed time, I gave it a few minutes and then called security. Something told me that he was the punctual type and since he wasn't there, I had the feeling something had gone wrong.

Indeed it had, and I found myself grateful when the doctor said he'd passed in his sleep, but sad for the loss that I was sure so many would feel.

I gathered all of his belongings and organized them so that I could ship them home. His wife received them, and not long after, she paid me a personal visit.

"It was so kind of you to make sure I got his things," she said, her eyes filled with tears. "I was already sad that I couldn't come with him on his last trip, but now I am sadder that I didn't."

"It was the least I could do," I told her. "The people that he met here will always remember him as quite a spunky and charming gentleman. He was my guest, and it was a pleasure to help serve him—and you—even to the end."

•   •   •

No, it's not all fun and games all the time in Las Vegas. In a town where the highest of highs coexist with the lowest of lows, there's a kind of odd, super-charged atmosphere that can sometimes tip people in the wrong direction.

Once, we had a pair of newlyweds who had been drinking and gambling all evening. The combination of too much excitement and too little sleep had obviously started to wear on them, and that night, they had their first fight as a married couple. It began loudly in the lobby and transcended the floors to their suite, from which other guests could hear a horrible ruckus. At one point, the wife suddenly realized that she had left her new wedding ring in the casino beside one of the slots.

She flung the door open and zoomed down several sets of stairs to come rushing up to the concierge desk, out of breath and begging for help. I gave her a bottle of water, and we began searching the casino for the ring. Thankfully, we were able to locate it quickly, and she thanked us profusely before she headed back up to their suite.

One never knows what deeper issues are at play with people, however, and when the wife got back into the room, she went into the bathroom to discover her husband hanging from his belt in the shower.

The woman ran screaming into the hall. Fortunately for them, a security guard had been sent to check things out. We'd received a number of phone calls from guests on that floor complaining about the yelling and noise. The guard rushed into the bathroom and cut her husband loose, saving his life and delivering him into the arms of his distraught new wife.

Normally, we would have to file a police report for this kind of event, but after much convincing by the wife, we agreed to record it as an internal hotel security matter only, and we were all thankful that a worse situation had been avoided.

Thank goodness this is not the usual kind of "loss" we're accustomed to dealing with in Vegas, but when it happens, the family needs someone there who can think calmly and help make arrangements. As a concierge, service sometimes transcends worldly bounds. I'm just glad we're there to help, even when the chips are down.

•   •   •

There are times when the best thing a concierge can do for a guest is to take excellent care of their children. Many years ago, a couple was married in our hotel. They were so pleased with their ceremony that they came to the hotel every year after, and as a result, we kindled a great friendship. A few years into their marriage, they had twins, and the trips to Vegas were foregone for a while, but before I knew it, they emailed to let me know they would be returning and were looking forward to seeing me and introducing me to the twins .

This would be the twins' first Vegas vacation, and I wanted to do something extra special for them. I went to the hotel kitchen and ordered a little surprise for them.

To the little boy went a strawberry covered in a white chocolate tuxedo design, and to the little girl went another chocolate-covered strawberry, wearing what appeared to be earrings and a necklace. It was such a small gesture, but the couple was really touched. They visited every year after, and each year, we'd create a new little his-and-her design for the twins. As little children, they received animals and other amusing designs, and as teenagers, they got credit card strawberries and iPhone designs, favorite baseball team logos or music icons. The family has gone so far as to put together a picture album with all the different designs we've come up with over the years, showing how we've watched these twins grow, while our love for this family has done the same.

•  •  •

Another time, a couple brought their daughter to Vegas to celebrate her twenty-first birthday. After all, Vegas is the perfect place to break in that ID in the various swanky nightclubs and casinos. Tricia just happened to be one of many guests celebrating their twenty-first birthdays with us, but her parents were extraordinary.

Of course, they wanted to make sure she had a wonderful time, but they also had specific surprises in mind to make this birthday even more memorable than anticipated. Tricia had a mild obsession with Louis Vuitton. She'd accumulated quite the collection of sunglasses, shoes, handbags, and other accessories, which she wore with pride. There wasn't an instance that I didn't see her with something Louis Vuitton on her person. Therefore, when it came to the cake, her parents already had a vision in mind.

Together, we conspired to have the hotel bakery design a special cake to look exactly like a Louis Vuitton bag, right down to the monogrammed insignia buckles and straps. At the stroke of midnight, when a bottle of champagne and the elaborate cake were delivered to her table in the nightclub, the brand new twenty-one-year-old was absolutely beside herself when she saw the lengths her parents (and concierge) had gone to.

It was a fabulous night, and the guests had a wonderful time—a birthday beyond being memorable. I think the most memorable thing to me was the price of the cake. At $2,000 it was costlier than the designer purse it was made to resemble!

• • •

But perhaps one of my favorite heartfelt memories was a father-daughter memory. I was handling a wedding for a woman I'd watched grow up and vacation with her family at our hotel for years and years. She was and always had been Daddy's little girl, and now that it was her wedding, she was trusting Daddy to set everything up, and he'd suggested having it with us. She loved the idea, and before we knew it, the wedding party had arrived, and the week was in full swing. We were handling everything, from the bachelor and bachelorette parties and the ceremony to the reception and honeymoon night. And nothing was too good for his little girl.

One day, the bride and I were going over a few details, and we sat down for a glass of complementary champagne. We began chatting about all the visits they'd made, and she elaborated on her childhood.

"Did you know me when I carried around that tattered Kermit the Frog?" she asked, and immediately, I was transported back years to when she, clad in the cutest sundresses, was bopping in and out of the lobby with a worn, green Kermit in her hands.

"He was my favorite," she told me. "I used to sing 'The Rainbow Connection' to my dad when I was little."

"You should do that at the reception," I suggested.

She smiled. "I don't know if I could get through it."

"What if we use that as the song for the father-daughter dance instead of 'Butterfly Kisses'? It's much more meaningful to you two."

She sat up straight. "It's a great idea. Do you think the DJ can find the song?"

"I'll make certain of it," already envisioning the tears in her father's eyes when he heard the music start up.

What she didn't know was that I was cooking up a little surprise for her, too. Glad to have a little extra time, I made a special order and had it delivered to the hotel the next day. On the night of the wedding, I pulled the bride to one side and handed her a gift bag.

"This is for your father," I explained.

"Why don't you give it to him?" she asked peering into the tissue paper.

"Because it's from you. Trust me." I smiled and patted her arm. I watched from afar as she took the gift bag and handed it to her father. His brow crinkled with curiosity as he dug through the tissue, but his eyes glistened with tears when he pulled out a brand new Kermit the Frog.

Neither of them was expecting it, and neither knew what the gift was, but when she saw what it was and how touched he was by it, the daughter cried alongside him.

Those are the best memories; the ones where you touch their hearts. All in all, my guests have provided me with years of stories, memories, and even some challenges. When it's all said and done, they've given me hundreds of thousands of reasons to love this job, and left lasting imprints on my heart.

# About the Author

When Hungarian native Mariann Mohos relocated to Las Vegas to pursue a Masters degree in Business Administration, she never imagined that she would one day also become one of the people who are integral to creating memorable experiences for the millions of guests visiting this spectacular and magical city each year.

For the past four years, Mohos has worked as a concierge at one of the major hotel and casino resorts in Las Vegas, where she has established herself as a trusted part of the concierge community.

Always fascinated by the inner workings of the hospitality industry, she has taken the opportunity to meet people from all walks of life, while still having ample time to pursue her own interests. With a command of four different languages, wide-ranging business experience in Europe and the US, and an outgoing personality, Mohos has found that serving as a concierge comes second nature to her.

Along with her love of Las Vegas, Mohos has an immense passion for learning and adores languages, traveling, the outdoors, and exploring different cultures. In addition to her MBA from the University Of Nevada, Las Vegas, she has degrees in English and Russian studies and Economics. Mohos founded and operated a grassroots marketing company for a number of years prior to beginning her career as a Las Vegas concierge.

# Acknowledgements

I would like to personally thank the following people, who have, in no small way, made a difference in my life, career, and in the writing of this book. To the concierges who gave their stories for this book, not only did you provide the essence of this collection, you have also reminded me over and over again why I love this business.

Zaida Banegas, you are truly the epitome of the perfect concierge. Your positive attitude, kindness, and compassion in the midst of any situation inspire me, and you are the ultimate 'people' person.

John Kasperowicz, there is no way to express how grateful I am for everything you have taught me and the kind of support that you have always given me. With regard to this book especially, you helped make it truly great. Not only professionally, but personally, you have been invaluable. I am eternally grateful to always know that you have my back.

Mike Sikalis, you have been more than a business partner to me. You have been a best friend, a mentor, and someone I deeply respect and admire. I have learned so many valuable things from you, especially that there is a shining opportunity in every challenge and I should never fail to look for it. This, and the other gems of wisdom I have picked up from you, have served me in writing this book and will continue to serve me for the rest of my life. Thank you.

Tom Antion, the amount of respect I have for you is monumental. Your integrity and work ethic is a great inspiration to me, and I would like to take this opportunity to thank you for guiding me through the creation of this book, from planting the first seed to harvesting and enjoying the finished product.

Gerry Culbert, René Vant 'Erve, Ken Stevens, Corinne Cunningham, and Dr. Mitch Mally, your help with this book has truly made it what it is, and I can't thank you enough.

To my friends, Andrea Meszaros, Katalin Pipicz, Eva Paczolay, Nikoletta Kroo, and Anita Babinszki, your input and encouragement has been very valuable, and has helped me make some of the best decisions I've made for this book. I will forever be grateful for your friendship, which has stood the test of time and distance. I have felt your support from Hungary the same as if you have been right beside me all along.

Lajos and Andrea Meszaros at Heribert C Bt, I am so thankful for your time and talent in perfecting this book's layout and overall design. You did such a great job!

To my editors, Samantha Cummings and Richard Horgan, my proofreader, Mirabella Mitchell, Annie Manning, book cover designer, and Aces Graphics, the cartoonists – thank you all for the hard work you've put into the book.

I've saved the very best for last. Thank you to my mother, who taught me from a very early age that every problem comes with a solution. You gave me the ability to skip the panicking and go straight to finding that solution. You also gave me the resilience to stand back up when I fall on my face – and that's something that has served me in this book and in countless other situations.

Thank you to my father. Because of you, I have learned important financial skills that have enabled me to live the kind of life I want, including creating this book. I've been fortunate enough not to struggle the way others have, even when my income wasn't that wonderful. I owe that to you, and I appreciate it very much.

I appreciate each and every one of you, and I hope the resulting product makes you all as proud as you make me.